THE SOUL'S JOURNEY

THE SOUL'S JOURNEY

By
HAZRAT PIR-O-MURSHID INAYAT KHAN

Edited and with a preface by
KORE SALVATO

OMEGA PUBLICATIONS
NEW LEBANON

Much of the material in *Soul's Journey* has previously been published in somewhat different form under the title *The Soul: Whence and Whither*. This new edition is based upon extensive scholarship re-creating the exact words that Hazrat Inayat Khan spoke, and is the most accurate of several versions. See the description of the publishing history of this material in the preface for more details.

Published by
OMEGA PUBLICATIONS
www.omegapub.com

Cover design by Hafizullah based on ideas by Yasodhara. Front cover art credits: *Head of Hypnos in Bronze* (British Museum) and *M51, the Whirlpool Nebula, NGC5194/5195* (by Christine Olson and Joe Lapre/Adam Block/ NOAO/AURA/NSF). Used with permission of the British Museum and the National Optical Astronomy Observatory. First edition financial support provided by Nurya Blood and Casey Blood. Production and publication support by Green Lion Press. Printed by Sheridan Books, Ann Arbor, Michigan.

This edition printed on acid-free paper that meets the American National Standards Institute Z39-48. Designed for durability and longevity with sewn binding, high-quality paper, and 15-point cover stock with lay-flat gloss film lamination.

Cataloging in Publication Data
Inayat Khan (1882–1927)
The Soul's Journey / Inayat Khan / edited by Kore Salvato.
Includes notes, bibliographical references, and index.
1. Sufism. 2. Psychology. 3. Mysticism. 4. Spirituality.
I. Inayat Khan II. Title
Library of Congress Control Number: 2003115274

10 9 8 7 6 5 4 3 2
Printed in the United States of America.
ISBN 978-0-930872-53-3

For more information on Sufism contact Sufi Order Internationsal
www.sufiorder.org

THE SOUL'S JOURNEY

v

Editor's Preface

Timely and timeless, our sustained interest in the soul—its nature, its progress, its place in daily life—shows that the soul matters to us. But what is this soul of ours exactly? And how can it go on a journey? Is it an adventure or an exile?

Pir-o-Murshid Inayat Khan (1882-1927), a great teacher in the Sufi tradition, had reflected on these questions since the early days of his own training with his murshid, or teacher, in Hyderabad, India. Commissioned by his teacher to go to the West to harmonize East and West with his music, Hazrat Inayat Khan first went to New York in 1910. Already a musician of great renown, he sang and played his vina for American audiences and, later, European ones, as far east as Russia. Gradually, he came to lecture extensively, and it is through these lectures that we, too, have access to that aspect of this teacher which is like music. That is to say that this series of lectures, given in the summer of 1923, has the attributes of music: lively, charming, ordered, resonant, surprising. There is no sternness here, no dogma to follow, no set of principles to which one must adhere.

Rather, it is the composition of a great master whose inner life involved deep contemplation on the nature of the soul, and whose destiny gave him the opportunity of offering the fruits of that inner study in the form of words. And although his native languages were Urdu and Gujarati, Hazrat Inayat Khan gave these lectures in English, which he had learned as a boy.

The value of studying this journey ourselves, according to Hazrat Inayat Khan, is that it calls our attention to the road along which we have to pass. Inayat Khan describes this journey, or the soul's progress, in three stages: the first is Towards Manifestation, in which the soul is moving into physical form; the second is Manifestation or physical existence; and the third is Towards the Goal, which is the return. The nature of the journey itself undergoes scrutiny in the conclusion to the series, in which Inayat Khan raises the question: "Is it a journey or is it not a journey?" And the answer: "It is a journey in fact, but not a journey in truth," suggests that the aspects of the journey are all appearances of the single, continuous, modulated existence of the soul.

Inayat Khan's initial meditations on the material which was to become a series of lectures delivered in 1923 in France began in Hyderabad. His murshid, Abu Hashim Madani, one day named the seven planes of manifestation in Arabic. That was all, just seven names. Taking these names as clues in his meditation, within three years Inayat Khan had experienced these planes. Perhaps it is this experience which prompts him to urge that we open our eyes so we may see for ourselves on this journey. Human beings make a great many mistakes, he says, but the principal mistake is that one goes through life thinking that one will be here forever. And so when the call comes, it comes as a blow rather than an invitation.

Indeed, that moment when death occurs is of great interest. Inayat Khan describes the soul at that particular moment. Whatever one's attitude is towards death, and the attitude of those around one at the moment of the soul's passing, the soul, he says, holds that impression—if it be an impression of the horror of death, the soul carries that with it. For this reason, it can be most helpful to know the terrain of one's spirit.

There is a Sufi story which Inayat Khan tells to illustrate this. A student went to his teacher and asked, "Tell me what is in heaven and what in hell." The teacher said, "Close your eyes and think of heaven." When he opened his eyes, the teacher asked him, "What did you see?" The student answered that he saw no sign of that paradise of which people speak—no beautiful plants and fruit, no things of comfort and luxury—he saw nothing. Then the teacher asked him to close his eyes again. When he finished his meditation, the teacher asked what he saw in hell. There, where the student had expected to see fire and people in torture, he saw nothing. The student asked, "What is the reason? Did I see or did I not see?" The teacher answered, "Certainly you have seen, but the jewels of paradise and the fire of hell, you have to take them for yourself. You do not find them there."

Knowledge of this journey, then, helps us to prepare for the hereafter. A follower of Hazrat Ali questioned him about the value of this preparation. The follower asked him, "What if our restraint leads us to nothing and there is no hereafter?" Ali answered, "If there is no hereafter, you and I are in the same boat. But if there is a hereafter, then I shall be better off."

Yet how does it help our lives here and now to know the nature of this journey?

Inayat Khan carefully addresses this question throughout the three parts of the series. The soul is unable to see itself; it thinks it is that which surrounds it. This mistake has, of course, important consequences, one of which Hazrat Inayat Khan illustrated in a story. There was a lion who lived among sheep since birth. This lion cavorted like the sheep and learned to bleat as they did. One day, another lion came upon this lion in the midst of the sheep. "Who are you?" the lion asked him. "A sheep," he answered. The second lion then took this lion to a nearby pool to show him his reflection. Only then did the young lion understand who he was.

The soul, which retains its impression of the angelic heavens, finds that impression buried under layers of illusion. When it begins its journey towards manifestation, every soul is an angel. The human being, however, is not less than that. The human being, Inayat Khan assures us, is a grown-up angel. This is a radical perspective in our age where divisions between people occur due to excessive nationalism, blind materialism, discontinuity between generations, and divisions so extreme that violence explodes too often. Criminals and victims—grown-up angels?

Inayat Khan does not avoid the difficult situations in which we might find ourselves in the course of our lives. At the end of one lecture, for example, someone asked, "Why are some souls born in miserable circumstances?" Inayat

Khan answers this, and then he poses the same question himself in a following lecture, and answers it again. And yet again. No one is accused of as much wrongdoing as God, Inayat Khan points out. If God is love, there is a way of understanding; if not with our minds, then with our souls. And what if it were true that each human being, even the most worthless, has a spark of the divine? Would we need to realign our thinking about ourselves, about our enemies? The joy of seeing ourselves, our God, our world in that light: that is the joy of uncovering the soul.

PUBLICATION HISTORY AND EDITORIAL PRACTICE

Probably most books published in the twentieth century do not have a complex editorial history. In the case of the present book, originally called *The Soul Whence and Whither*, however, this edition already represents the sixth editing of the lectures presented here. The lectures themselves were given during the Sufi summer school in Suresnes, France, in the summer of 1923, carefully taken down in shorthand by a Dutch mureed, Sakina Furnée, whom Inayat Khan assigned the important task of recording his lectures.

The first edition of the book appeared in 1924, printed in Southampton, England. Exactly how and by whom this first edition was prepared remains controversial, but that text differed considerably from the accurate shorthand record. The first edition also contained a most unfortunate error. In the concluding lecture of the series, Inayat Khan poses the important question about the soul's journey: "Is it a journey or is it not a journey?" And he answers the question, as we have discussed, "It is a journey in fact, but not a journey in truth." The first edition omitted a line of type so that the answer was mistakenly truncated to read "It is a journey in truth." Inayat Khan felt that the whole book had been spoiled. He proposed that the word "not" be inserted with ink or a rubber stamp, and, in fact, in a copy of the newly published book he had the words, "It is not a journey objectively," inserted in handwriting.

An errata list was inserted into the books, containing the phrase "It is not a journey objectively," and in 1927 a revised edition corrected some of the errors. However, Murshida Sherifa Goodenough, Inayat Khan's designated editor, left a note indicating that a new edition was needed.

That new edition had to wait thirty-three years, and when it was made, no new manuscript was used, but rather further editorial revisions were introduced into the existing text. The line in the Conclusion appears as: "It is not a journey in truth," restoring half of what Inayat Khan actually said. This was the 1960 edition, which began the series of volumes called *The Sufi Message of Hazrat Inayat Khan*. Another edition in 1977 from Sufi Order Publications (now named Omega Publications) reproduced the first edition exactly, including the errors. In 1984, a new edition from East-West Publications referred to a range of documents from the Summer School of 1923 and included many of the questions and answers for the first time. The Conclusion in this edition reads, "It is not a journey objectively," with a footnote referring to the editorial history.

Then in 1988 the first volume of a new series, *The Complete Works of Pir-o-Murshid Hazrat Inayat Khan* appeared, and, as this volume included the entire summer school of 1923, it contained all the lectures which constituted *The Soul: Whence and Whither*. This series gives priority to the oldest available version of the lectures of Inayat Khan and indicates variations in other manuscripts, including the first edition, in footnotes. In many cases, these are unedited records, transcripts made from the shorthand reportings commissioned by Inayat Khan so that his exact words would be recorded.

This present edition is based on *The Complete Works*, and therefore keeps as close as possible to the spoken word, relying primarily on the shorthand reportings of Sakina Furnée, and, when those are not available, the shorthand reportings of Kismet Stam, one longhand reporting of

Murshida Sherifa Goodenough, and many questions and answers from Sirdar Van Tuyll, Kefayat Lloyd, and Murshida Sophia Green—all students of Inayat Khan who were present at the 1923 summer school. In accord with the text of the *Complete Works*, the present edition restores the conclusion as it was originally spoken.

Why this emphasis on the spoken word?

Hazrat Inayat Khan himself gave this direction when he urged, "Do not change my words, form or phrase unless it is most necessary. Even so, most carefully avoid all changes which can be avoided. Otherwise you might lose the sense of my teaching, which is as essential to the message as the perfume in the rose. If the form in which I give my teaching seems to you not as correct as it ought to be from a literary point of view, do not mind; let it be my own language. There will come a time when there will be a search for my own words. Just now if my words are not accepted as the current coin, they will always be valued as the antique."

This direction presents a unique challenge for an editor. The changes which we have sought to avoid in the present edition include substituting one seemingly better word for the one actually said, such as when the hereafter is compared to the autumn of the soul and previous editors have changed the word "autumn" to "winter." Other changes to be avoided include a change in word order, omissions of words, phrases, and even sentences, as well as the addition of words, poems, and editorial explanations.

There are, however, changes which need to be made in order to make a presentation in standard English. Occasionally these changes do, in fact, require a change in word order, the omission or addition of articles, and other clarifications such as supplying the noun in a series of pronoun references. Even these necessary changes can be problematical. In a chapter on the subject of manifestation, for example, Hazrat Inayat Khan speaks about experience. He says that a person "takes the essence and then it is all thrown away." Subsequent editions substitute the words "the rest" for the pronoun. Perhaps the passage is more interesting if the "it" is left to puzzle over. In addition, gaps occur in the manu-script, particularly in the questions and answers; sometimes the meaning there can be inferred and the word is supplied for uninterrupted reading,

This editing is not intended to replace the verbatim tran-scripts. Rather, it is to make a readable written text from material delivered as lectures. The great advantage of work-ing with *The Complete Works* is that in addition to compiling the original transcripts, this series presents Hazrat Inayat Khan's lectures in chronological order. In the summer of 1923, for example, when the lectures originally called *The Soul Whence and Whither* were given, Hazrat Inayat Khan gave as many as three lectures in one day on various topics such as the personality. In the questions and answers, par-ticularly in these other sessions, there was a spillover of interest from the themes presented in the lectures on the soul. The relevant questions and answers from those other sessions have been included here.

The chronology of the lectures in this text follows the earliest editions. The series begins on August 10 and goes through September 19. This chronology is interrupted by eleven additional lectures given earlier in the summer (July 2 through August 1) called metaphysics; these lectures, on the subject of manifestation, are included at the end of Part II, as in the earlier editions. One of these lectures, on the sub-ject of breath, was apparently overlooked in preparing the first edition, and has been included as part of *The Soul* here for the first time. (The lecture itself has been published in the Gatha series, but the six questions and answers follow-ing the lecture, which along with many other questions and answers appeared for the first time in *The Complete Works*, are included in the present book.)

New material is most evident in the inclusion of all the questions and answers given at the end of each of the lec-tures. These questions and answers are not rearranged or grouped together in a seemingly more logical placement. As a result, sub-themes emerge in the question and answer sessions, which are occasionally continued from session to session and are sometimes interwoven into the text of the lectures themselves, almost like the parts of a musical composition. The theme of justice, for example, occurs contrapuntally throughout the book.

A point worth making is that Hazrat Inayat Khan's wife was an American, born in New Mexico, and he was influenced at least to a degree by her idiom. He used the phrase, "sawing logs," for example, for someone sleeping, meaning of course, snoring, a meaning not easily available to the highly talented European linguists who have wrestled with the editorial issues of transcribing Inayat Khan's lectures. In addition, studies in America on the question of editorial changes with regard to gender in Inayat Khan's texts suggest that in some cases, the word "we", which was the word originally said, was changed to the more formal "one" or "man." Now that editorial fashion is more flexible, that which once seemed necessary to change in editorial practice no longer seems so.

However, in the area of gender neutral language, there is a call in America and Australia to change pronoun references from "he" to a more inclusive "we" or "they." Because the aim of this edition is to remain as faithful to the spoken text as the dictates of standard written English allow, we have not altered the text to change the masculine pronoun references. I think, however, it is important to assume inclusiveness on the part of Inayat Khan to the extent of substituting the female pronoun reference in one's reading if one wishes to do so. Indeed, in Urdu, one of Inayat Khan's original languages, the pronoun *woh* refers to he, she, it, and that.

Finally, an extensive index allows for a comprehensive exploration of subjects of interest to the reader.

We have followed the current standard style of capitalization, in which only nouns for God and not pronoun references are capitalized.

Kore Salvato
Suresnes, May 2003

EDITOR'S ACKNOWLEDGMENTS

Heartfelt thanks to Vakil Nancy Wilkinson, Associate Editor, for her apt and timely correction of the scanned texts and her clear editorial suggestions. Abi'l-Khayr of Omega Publications likewise presented graceful solutions to a number of editorial problems. The late Marci Wennergren helped us avoid several errors through her careful proof-reading of the text. My husband, Donald A. Sharif Graham, who has edited a variety of texts of Pir-o-Murshid Inayat Khan, debated points of usage and prepared the extensive index. The late Munira van Voorst van Beest, the founding editor of *The Complete Works of Pir-o-Murshid Hazrat Inayat Khan*, first suggested that I undertake this task. Kashfinur Heine provided technical support. The Demeter Foundation offered generous financial support.

Kore Salvato

THE SOUL'S JOURNEY

Hazrat Pir-o-Murshid Inayat Khan

Introduction

INTRODUCTION

BEFORE the manifestation, what did exist? *Zat*, the essence, the truly existing, the only being. In what form? In no form. As what? As nothing. The only definition that words can give is: the Absolute. In the Sufi terms this existence is termed *ahdiat*.

Consciousness arose out of this Absolute, the consciousness of existence. There was nothing of which the Absolute could be conscious, only of its existence. This stage is called *wahdan*. Out of this consciousness of existence a feeling developed, a feeling that "I" exist. It was a development of the consciousness of existence. It is this development which formed the ego, the logos which is termed *wahdaniat* by the Sufis. With the feeling of the "I-ness", the innate power of the Absolute, so to speak, pulled itself together. In other words, concentrated on one point. Thus the all-pervading radiance formed its center, the center which is the divine spirit or the light. In Sufi terms it is called *arwah*.

This centered light then divided existence into two forms, the light and darkness. In fact there is no such thing as darkness; there has never been darkness; it is only more light compared with less light. This light and darkness formed an *akasha*, in Sufi terms, *asman*, an accommodation, a mold. And the phenomenon of light and shade, working through this mold, furthered the manifestation into a great many accommodations, *asmans* or akashas. Every step manifestation has taken, a variety of forms has been the result and it is the plane of definite forms of nature which is called in the Sufi terminology, *ajsam*. Out of these forms gradually came: from the mineral, the vegetable kingdom; from the vegetable, the animal kingdom; and from the animal, the human race. Thus the divine spirit was provided the *arwah*, the bodies which it has needed from the time it centered itself on one point and from there spread its rays as various souls.

Besides the phenomenon of four elements—*baad,* the air; *atish*, the fire; *aab*, the water; *khaak*, the earth—there is one, the ether, which is the source and goal of all the elements, making them five. These elements have worked in consonance with one another and against one another in order to bring about the results desired by the divine wisdom working behind them. In every *akasha* or *asman,* they have been more or less present; one without the others did not exist. The four together brought the fifth. In this way the whole manifestation has taken place through a gradual process of development.

Manifestation has half finished its task in the creation of man, in whom is born the wisdom of controlling and realizing all that is on the earth to its best advantage. And in man the purpose of manifestation is fully accomplished, especially in such a man who has on his return journey become more and more conscious of his purpose by widening his outlook and by living a fuller life; the man who has reached that stage of realization which is called divinity, in which is the fulfillment of the purpose of this whole manifestation.

Thus six definite steps towards manifestation are recognized by the Sufis. The first three are called *tanzih,* and next three are called *tashbih.* The first three are imperceptible; the next three distinguishable.

* * *

Question: *The first condition of consciousness which is unconscious is impossible for the human mind to grasp, is it not?*

Answer: Certainly it is. But it is possible for the soul to understand it. If it were not so, the revelation would not have been possible. The revelation comes not only as an inspiration, but it comes as a soul's experience and therefore, it is. For the mind it is impossible to understand, but for the soul it is its own experience.

Question: *Why is the moon used as a symbol and not the sun?*

Answer: Both are used as symbols for different purposes, the sun as well as the moon. The sun for power, the moon for inspiration.

Question: *What language are* zat, baad, khaak?

Answer: They come from an Hebraic origin, Arabic and Persian words, which have been used by Sufis of the ancient times.

Question: *What is the definite stage in creation when God breathed his spirit into man?*

Answer: It is that definite stage of creation which is recognized by the Sufis as *Insaan,* which was mentioned just now. This was the period when Adam was born, when the creation of man took place.

Question: *Before manifestation did not the being of God exist as a trinity in unity?*

Answer: Before manifestation the being of God existed as all. All in it: unity, trinity, duality, no duality, it was not distinct. If it were not there, how would it have come? It all existed. But beyond and above, what existed? God, the only being. The knowledge of two, three, four, five is for us, for our benefit, for us to understand things better. But the real knowledge is the knowledge of unity, one, the only being.

Question: *Were the four elements part of the manifestation, the life of the only being?*

Answer: They are all the outcome. Duality is the outcome of manifestation. In the origin there is unity, oneness; all duality is manifestation.

Question: *We hear them spoken of as great beings.*

Answer: These four powers are great powers which work

through all planes of existence, and which play their role in every form.

Question: *As thought necessitates movement or mental action, it is difficult to see how it arose in the Absolute before the manifestation.*

Answer: Thought did not rise in the Absolute. It was the consciousness which was its predisposition, which was in it, in its being, that awoke. Just like a person who is asleep, it does not mean that it is not his disposition to wake up; it is his nature to wake up, but he wakes up from the sleep. The awakening was the first impulse towards manifestation. That distinct impulse is called *wahdat*. But to understand these two distinct planes is a rather difficult thing, because it is most fine and delicate. There is a difference between *wahdat* and *wahdaniat*. To become conscious is one thing, and to become self-conscious is another thing. One person is asleep, just a little awake; a little noise would tell him something is going on. Still, he is not self-conscious yet, that comes when he is wider awake. *Wahdat*: when the Absolute became conscious. *Wahdaniat*: when the Absolute became wide awake and felt his being as "I am." That action brought about the power of breathing in, that is the pulling oneself together. As soon as he thought "I am," he became a conscious existence for himself as "I am." Therefore, it is the *logos*.

Question: *Are not all five elements in their essence colorless?*

Answer: In the essence everything is colorless. The nearer to the essence, the less color there is. But it is the color by which they are distinguished in the outer planes.

Question: *Has the manifestation reached the same point in evolution throughout the whole universe or are there various stages of manifestation at the same time and place?*

Answer: Yes, various stages in different places. Some more advanced and some less.

Question: *Was there then ever a period of time when there*

6

was no consciousness in the absolute being of God, no life anywhere?

Answer: Silent consciousness. We cannot call silent consciousness no consciousness. If there were no consciousness there would never have been a consciousness. It was the development of the consciousness of the only being which brought the self-consciousness. Out of the silent or deep consciousness the only being arose and came to self-consciousness.

THE SOUL'S JOURNEY

TOWARDS MANIFESTATION

THE MANIFESTED SOUL

TOWARDS THE GOAL

THE SOUL
TOWARDS MANIFESTATION

1

THE DIVINE SPIRIT is known by the mystics of all ages as the sun, and, therefore, in all ancient mystical symbols the sun has been pictured as the sign of God. This conception gives one a help in the further knowledge of metaphysics.

The sun is that aspect of the absolute God in which God begins to manifest, and his first step towards manifestation is his contraction, that contraction which is seen in all living beings and in all objects. It is first contraction that takes place and next expansion. The former tendency is the desire of inhalation and the latter of exhalation. The contraction and expansion which is seen in all aspects of life comes from God himself.

The omnipotent life, by this tendency, became concentrated, and it is this concentrated light of intelligence which is the sun recognized by the mystics. Shamsi Tabriz[1] mentions this in his verses. He says, "When the sun of his countenance became manifest, the atoms of both worlds began to appear as his light fell, and every atom was adorned with a name and a form." In the Vedanta the Hindus have called it Chaitanya, the spirit or the light of God. In the Qur'an it is mentioned, "We have made thy light out of our light and from that light we have made the whole universe."

In plain words this explains that when there was nothing,

no form, no name, no person, no object, there was intelligence, and it is the contraction of that intelligence which brought its essence into a form of light, which is called the Divine Spirit. The expansion of the same light has been the cause of the whole manifestation. In plain words, manifestation is the exhalation of God, and what is called *Laya*, destruction, the end of the world, is the inhalation of God. The Divine Spirit spreads itself, which we call manifestation, containing various names and forms; and God contracts himself, which humanity dreads and calls destruction.

For this many blame God, many judge him and many think it unfair on the part of God to create and destroy. But for God, who is the only being, this is the natural condition by which he eternally lives. The beginning and the end of the world is only his one breath, the duration of which is numberless years. Between this one breath myriads of lives have been born, lived and died and have experienced this world and that world, heaven and the contrary place, all.

Souls, therefore, are the rays of this sun, which is called in Sanskrit, *Brahmani*, and the nature of the ray is to extend and withdraw, to appear and disappear, and the duration of its existence is incomparably short when considered with the duration of the eternal God, the Divine Spirit. There are living creatures, small germs and worms and insects, who do not live longer than a moment; and there are other beings whose life is for a hundred years and some creatures who live longer still; and yet it is a moment, even if it were a thousand years, compared with eternity.

The time that man knows is in the first place learned by the knowledge of his own physical constitution. The Sanskrit word *pala*, which means moment, has come from the pulse which beats; it comes from pulsation. This knowledge has been completed to some extent by the study of nature: the changes of the seasons and the rounds that the world makes around the sun; by these man has completed his idea of time. Many wish to limit divine law to this man-made conception of time and make speculations about it. But the tendency of the mystic is to bend his head low in worship as the thought of the eternal life of God, the only being, comes to his mind. Instead of questioning why and what about it, he contemplates upon the being of God, and so raises his consciousness above the limitations of time and space, so liberating his soul by lifting it to the divine spheres.

* * *

Question: *What relation does the destruction of form during manifestation have to the great breath? Does it affect it at all?*

Answer: No, it does not affect the great breath except as a shadow which is reflected in the divine sun and mirrored upon every existing being. For an instance, when one person dies, every soul in the world feels it, some consciously, and most unconsciously, in accordance to their closeness or distance to that particular soul. But it does not rob the Divine Spirit of its power and wisdom, as the ebb and flow of the sea is not at all affected by the waves, whether the wave goes this way or that way. But the manifestation is the same, all through manifestation, from the beginning to the end and from God to the smallest atom. For instance, as God breathes so we breathe, and so the animals and birds. Now the scientist has brought proof that the trees breathe the same breath in the ebb and flow … .

When one sees that contraction and expansion, which goes on in the whole universe in the same manner as it has begun, then one sees that in the whole creation, with its various aspects and all the difference there is in the nature and character of things and beings, there is one law and one manner in which the whole creation takes place and goes on to its finish.

Question: *Can you explain to us more why God inhales and exhales?*

Answer: Yes, if not, we could not exist. The condition of existing is inhaling and exhaling. So God exists also, only his inhaling is the end of the whole creation. But we say that it is a harm done to us. But is it unfair if we breathe? It may be unfair to many little germs. Such lives are destroyed

13

while we are breathing. Also, there are lives that by our breathing are created. There will come a time when science will find out that the breath of man is creative, not only of atmosphere, but also of life; it is a living being. At the root of this secret one will find the reason for all disease. It [breath] is creative as a living being. Science now finds that behind every disease there is a germ of disease. There will come a time when one will find out that it all comes from inhaling and exhaling. As God creates, so man creates by his breath.

Question: *What is the difference between what God inhales and what he exhales?*

Answer: The difference is in the character, in the nature [of the breath]. His exhaling is creative, his inhaling is destructive. His inhaling is Shiva, the exhaling Brahma.

Question: *Is the destruction which takes place at the end of the inhaling sudden or gradual?*

Answer: It is gradual, as we inhale and exhale. At the finishing of the breath the destruction is finished. But a little picture of this is the life of very large cobras. There are stories of some people having seen very large cobras, cobras in whose mouth even a cow or a buffalo could enter. In six months or a year's time, when they are hungry, they have only to open their mouth, and to take a breath, and if there is a cow, it is attracted and goes into the mouth of the cobra. The cobra eats it and then sleeps for six months or a year. This is a legend or a story.

I myself have noted a large cobra eating a chicken, not in part, all at once. One would never have thought that a cobra could eat a whole chicken. Then the cobra's power is great because it is meditative. In all mystical symbols the cobra has been made a mystical sign, because there is so much that one can learn from the life of a cobra. It fasts for a long time because it takes time to assimilate. Not so greedy as a dog, it does not run after its food, it attracts food. Then the patience of the cobra is wonderful. It is the same picture.

14

Therefore, mystics have given in the ancient mysticism the cobra in all their symbols. The whole manifestation is attracted to that Divine Spirit. In the Qur'an it is said that, "All has come from God and to him all will return."

Question: *[Question not recorded.]*

Answer: When the serpent has the tail in its mouth, it means perfection. Man and God are the two ends of the line.

Question: *What is the real significance of the word nirvana?*

Answer: The word *nirvana* means no *vana*, which means difference, distinction. When there is no difference, no distinction, that is *nirvana*. When one has risen above.

Question: *You named contraction and inhalation together, but speaking physically, is [question incomplete]?*

Answer: The effect of inhaling is that it has an effect upon the heart to expand, and when one exhales the effect is to contract. But really speaking, the effect is the outcome, not the action. It is the action of contraction which produces that [inhalation] of the [breath], and it is the expansion [that produces exhalation]; it is on the contrary.

We see this tendency in all beings, in the octopus, in the insects. When sheep fight, they also contract themselves first, then manifestation comes. The same tendency is in the elephants: they first contract, then all strength is [manifest].

We exhale what we inhale. If we inhale and keep ourselves in a better state, our exhaling would also become a healing. For instance, a person who wants to take revenge, who wants to harm another, when he inhales the breath becomes poison; in his breath he has already created numberless germs of illness, which will disturb his own life and those who come into his atmosphere. Also think of those who are inclined to kindness and love, whose aspiration is for goodness and who have good thoughts. Their inhaling and exhaling will be uplifting and healing; wherever the vibrations are moving, it will all be their healing atmosphere.

Breath is not only physical; it touches the deepest part of

our being. What we know is only inhaling and exhaling, what we feel through the nostrils. That is not breath. Breath is that power which makes our lives, which connects body with soul and mind. Breath, in point of fact, is a rosary.

2

THE SOUL, which is the ray of the divine sun in one sphere, the sphere in which it does not touch any earthly being, is called angel. Therefore, every soul passes through the angelic plane. In other words, every soul is an angel before it touches the earthly plane. It is angels who become human beings, and those who do not become human beings remain angels. A human being, therefore, is a grown-up angel, and an angel, therefore, is a soul who never grew up.

Infants, who come on earth with their angelic qualities and sometimes pass away without having experienced the life of the grown-up man, show us the same picture of the original condition of the soul. The idea that the angels are nearer to God, according to this doctrine, is right. Souls who have not journeyed further are naturally close to the Divine Spirit; they are angels.

Someone asked the Prophet[2] why man was greater than the angels, man who causes all the bloodshed on the earth compared with angels who always occupy themselves in the praise of God. The answer was that the angels knew not anything of the earth. They knew God and so they occupied themselves with God. But man is greater, for when he comes on earth, he has much to occupy himself with in the world and still he pursues God.

That angelic sphere is pure of passions or emotions which are the source of all wrong and sin. Souls, pure of all greed and desires that the denseness of earth gives, are angels who know nothing else but happiness, for happiness is the real nature of the soul. The Hindus call angels *suras*. *Sura* means breath also, and breath means life. *Suras*, therefore, mean pure lives, lives that live long. In the Hindu scriptures there is another word used, *asura*, meaning lifeless; in other words mortals whose lives have been caught in the net of mortality.

Man may continue to retain the angelic quality even in his life on the earth as a human being, and it is the angelic quality which can be traced in some souls who show innocence and simplicity in their lives, which is not necessarily foolishness. It only shows the delicacy of a flower in a personality together with fragrance. Angelic souls are inclined to love, to be kind, and to be dependent upon those who show them some love. They are ready to believe, willing to learn, inclined to follow that which seems to them for the moment good, beautiful and true.

The picture of the angels as we read in the scriptures, sitting upon the clouds and playing on harps, is but an expression of a mystic secret. Playing the harp is vibrating harmoniously. One can see that in a person who is vibrating harmoniously his presence becomes the inspiration of music and poetry. The person whose heart is tuned to the pitch of the angelic spheres will show on earth heavenly bliss. Therefore, the wise seek the association of spiritual beings. And sitting on the clouds only means that the angels are above all clouds. The clouds are for the beings of the dense earth. They are free from the momentary pleasures and continued spells of depression. Clouds do not touch them; they are above clouds.

The souls who are in direct touch with the spirit of God, who have no knowledge of the false world which is full of illusions, who live and know not death, whose lives are happiness, whose food is divine light, make around this Divine Spirit, which is called *nur* by the Sufis, an aura which is called the highest heaven.

* * *

Question: *What about the angels who remain angels?*

Answer: They are in their highest glory.

Question: *Have the angels not any contribution or relation to human life?*

Answer: They have, as that of a little child and a grown-up person.

Question: *What is the meaning of the angels who in the stories of the Old Testament appear to man? Were they real apparitions?*

Answer: That angel is called *Farishta*, "who is sent," and they are as real as they can be intelligible to those to whom they are sent.

Question: *In how far do angels help the human being?*

Answer: As far as an infant can help a grown-up person.

Question: *What causes some beings to become mortal and some to remain angels?*

Answer: It is the strength with which the mechanism was wound. One clock goes on for the whole month, and the other clock wants winding after twenty-four hours. There is another clock which can go on for a whole year. So is the whole mechanism of the whole of life. There are some beings, souls, which can go on much longer because the winding is stronger; some shorter because the force that is at the back of it is only that much.

It does not mean that the angels were meant to be angels, not to go further, but it happens that the soul who goes so far and only remains in that heaven [*sentence incomplete*]. There are other souls who have a greater power to go further; they have gone to the angelic sphere and go farther still by the power with which they have first started. It is like the hoop of a child: it can go ten, twenty or more circles. It is in their striking of the stick. That striking is the work of God, the inner working of that Divine Spirit.

Question: *What gives them the start? Why some have [question incomplete]?*

Answer: If it is natural for a little child that every time he strikes his hoop it will not go as far as it went first, so it is with that natural movement which comes from the Divine Spirit that strikes one to go further than another. If we study the light, we shall find that all the rays do not go evenly; some go very far, others remain very near the flame. Every ray, large or small, has a different distance to which it reaches.

Question: *What causes some beings to become mortal and some to remain angels?*

Answer: It is the mortal garb that they take, and therefore it is the garb which is mortal; they are not mortal. Upon the consciousness of the soul it becomes impressed. It is the garb which the soul has adopted for its use. As every person begins by thinking, "I am my body," and from that time in the illness of the body thinks, "I am ill," and the death of the body means, "I am dead" to that person, then he becomes his garb; he is not himself. If there is any illusion, it is this.

Question: *Are souls angels from the very beginning of their journey towards manifestation?*

Answer: Yes, since all has come from God, then all has come from the divine light. The first offshoot of the divine light is an angel.

Question: *Do they experience life on each succeeding plane of existence towards the physical life?*

Answer: Yes, they do, but not all. For instance, imagine a picture of a thousand birds starting from Paris to go to England. Some were able to go as far as Rouen. There they liked the place, they stayed there, they enjoyed it, they forgot all. Some went to Le Havre and they enjoyed the seashore, and just lived there and were happy. Some went still further, crossed the Channel, and arrived in England. Those who stayed in Rouen, they had not a very long journey to come back to Paris again. Those who had crossed, for them it was a very long journey to come back.

Question: *Do angels have a form before they reach the physical plane?*

Answer: It is a question which is very subtle and most difficult to explain in words. The reason is that every thing or being that has a name has a form. But we are accustomed only to call something which we can see a form, and what our eyes cannot see we do not call it a form. And to conceive the form of an angel what is wanted is to turn into an angel in order to conceive what the true angelic form is. But we are accustomed to picture every one like us, and therefore whenever we think of fairies or angels, spirits or ghosts, we picture them very like us. The fairies of the Chinese have more the Chinese figure, and the fairies of the Russians have Russian hats, because the mind will picture what it is accustomed to.

Question: *When they appear in a vision?*

Answer: Yes, they always will put [sentence incomplete]. The vision itself will be covered under that form in which man is accustomed to see it.

Question: *Are souls on their return from the physical plane also called angels?*

Answer: No, they are called spirits.

Question: *On returning does the soul also go to the angelic sphere?*

Answer: Yes, it does; in that case there are different names used for that.

Question: *What is the opposite of the angels which are by some called evil spirits? Are they fallen angels?*

Answer: If the angel fell, it would not be an angel, because the angel should fall to the earth. And as soon as it touched the earth, it would not be an angel any longer.

An evil spirit is quite a different thing. It is a word which is applied to a soul who has passed from the earth who has collected through life all evil.

3

THE SOULS in the angelic sphere have all goodness, and this proves that goodness is natural; and what is contrary to our nature we call it badness. The souls in the angelic sphere are innocent. This also shows that innocence is the natural condition of the soul, and the lack of innocence is a foreign element which the soul acquires after coming on earth. In the angelic sphere the souls are happy; this shows that unhappiness does not belong to souls. It is something which is foreign to the soul. Therefore, the discomfort gives unhappiness.

Souls on the earth have something of the angelic quality; therefore, they readily respond and are attracted without resistance to the innocence, happiness and goodness of another person. If they knew that it is because this is the original quality of their soul, they would develop the same in their own being. As Rumi[3] has said, "People are drawn towards me and they shed tears with me, cry, and yet they know not what it is in me that attracts them." Seeking after goodness, innocence and happiness helps the angelic qualities to develop in a soul. Spirituality, therefore, is the development of the angelic quality and love of spirituality is the longing for the angelic spheres. It is homesickness.

Does death frighten spiritual beings? No, death for the spiritual soul is only a gate, a door, through which it enters into that sphere which every soul has known to be its home. Souls who become conscious of the angelic sphere, even to the smallest degree, hear the calling of that sphere, and if they have any discomfort in this world, it is that homesickness which the call of the angelic sphere gives.

The soul may be likened to a ray of the sun; so the souls of angels, not being adorned with physical garb, are lights, are flames themselves. The scriptures therefore say the angels are made of light, *nur. Nur* is especially that light which comes from the divine sun, the spirit of God. In short, all souls are made of that essence which is the essence of the whole manifestation, and in every soul there exists some part of that essence, however little. The quality of that essence is to absorb all else which is around it in time and to develop, so that it would emerge in its own element, which is divine.

* * *

Question: *The soul coming on earth is the angel; if a soul coming on earth is affected by the spirits, from the returning spirits, why are not all the angels affected by those spirits?*
Answer: A sphere means a certain limit, a certain horizon, that in that horizon nothing dense or earthly can enter. Before it enters it must become melted. And therefore the souls in those spheres are not touched by any souls coming from the earth. No souls coming from the earth are allowed to enter that sphere before they are purified of all elements of denseness. An example, very well known in India, is the story of Indra. It is a story which has been made into dramas and operas and produced for ages. The people of India have never become tired of it. It is always new and very interesting because it has interest for the ordinary mind and for the thinking mind, both.

The story is that a prince was taken up into heaven by a fairy who loved him, and the prince urged the fairy to take him to the court of Indra where she was appointed to dance every day. The fairy refused because, she said, "No earthly being is allowed to enter into heaven. I have already done something against the rule. To bring you into the court of Indra will be the end of your life." He said, "I will not listen. I must see where you go." She said, "If you wish it, I will take you."

She took him to the court of Indra where she was

appointed to dance. She told him to hide behind her wings. But the wings could not cover, and those who saw told Indra that a man from the dense earth, who was not allowed to come to heaven, had been brought by this fairy. And the wrath of Indra arose, and he said, "I will cast you down, the fairy who was privileged to be in heaven, that you should live a life in the wilderness, a life of loneliness for many years to come. And for this man another sphere of wilderness. And not until you will be purified of the five elements, will you be able to enter the spheres of heaven."

Well, it is an allegorical story. The fairy was the soul, and the man is the body. They were separated, because in heaven there is no place for both body and soul. The place of the body is only on the earth; it has no place there. And however much the soul tries to take body to heaven, there is no place there. The soul was also cast out, because it loved the body so much. When they are purified of the five elements: no longer of fire, earth, water, air [and ether], then only the angel remains, the human goes away. What remains? The angel only.

Question: *The soul that goes back, does it go back rich? Does it develop spiritually?*

Answer: It is spiritual already. Why has it come? To get the experience of the earthly spheres. And then to lose it? Yes, there is nothing in it. It is to come from innocence to virtue, and to be purified from it; from virtue to innocence again.

Question: *Will you give us a definition of what initiation is, and what of ordination? Also explain more about the two different ways of working?*

Answer: Initiation is that which is given in the Sufi Movement in the circle called the Sufi Order. Ordination is that which is given in the Sufi Movement in the circle called the Church of All, or the Universal Worship. By this ordination a person is made a *cherag*, whose responsibility it is to serve God and humanity in the path of religion.

It is a question which can be answered in many volumes,

25

the ways of working. In short, one can say that devotion and love is the most desirable path, which welcomes every soul, and by which every soul is blessed. That is the work of the *cherag*. The path of initiation has its many aspects. The patient soul going through different aspects attains to the desired goal.

Question: *Why is there less of the essence of the spirit of God in one soul than in another? Do we not all come on earth with the same quantity of that essence?*

Answer: No, God is not so inartistic. Even in the tree, every fruit is different; every flower on the same plant is different. And if there were no difference, there would have been no joy in life. Life is interesting because of the differences.

Question: *Then the soul who has less to begin with, is it handicapped?*

Answer: No one is handicapped in life. Life is progressing. Some have more to begin with and less in the end.

Question: *When one is purged of the five elements, are all the souls then equal?*

Answer: Still there is a variation. Where there is duality, there is variation. Where there are two, there is variation. When there are two flames they are not alike though they are of the same element. In truth there is one, but in fact there are two.

Question: *If the soul keeps its angelic qualities on earth and does not experience earthly passions and other experiences of the earth, why does it come on earth? Is it only to be an example to others?*

Answer: If you think so, yes. No one lives without action, and every action has its meaning. And therefore no one has come here without a purpose. If the meaning of his life and action we cannot understand, it does not mean that that person has not come for a purpose. And, therefore, in sum total of the whole working of the universe, every individual seems to have filled a certain place which was meant for him and has been of a certain use in the whole working of the universe. No one in this world is useless.

One person who sits in the midst of the crowd and is busy the whole day, and another person who has gone from the world and no one has seen him, even he is busy; they all are busy. The most occupied and the most lazy, the most useful and the most useless, they all have their part to perform in this drama of life. The only difference between the wise and everyone is this: that everyone does not know the secret, the meaning of life. The wise learns his wisdom in learning to understand the meaning of life.

Question: *What does initiation mean?*

Answer: Initiation means entering into a vow, a trust and confidence, in order to know and understand the life which is beyond the conception of everybody. Of course, as one goes further in the path of initiation, the higher one reaches in one's understanding. Every soul, after having reached a certain stage, receives an initiation. Some are initiations which the soul does not know, and yet it is a step further in life. But the real initiations begin when the soul knows that it is being initiated.

Ordination is the service of God. When God wishes a soul to serve in his path, an ordination comes. One thing is the unfoldment of the soul, the other thing is the utilizing of the life, using the life to its best purpose.

4

THE SOUL going towards manifestation, which is still in the angelic spheres, is free from all differences and distinctions which are the conditions of the soul's life on earth. Are angels male and female? This question can be answered that the dual aspect starts even from the angelic spheres. God alone is above this aspect, but in all other conditions and aspects of life this aspect is to be seen, though this difference is more distinct on the earth plane. In the angelic plane it is not distinguishable.

And now there is another question: Are the angels in touch with people on earth? And the answer is that their life does not necessitate any communication with human life on earth, except some who are destined to perform a certain duty on the earth. There is mentioned in the ancient scriptures that an angel came with a message to the prophets of Beni Israel. But the explanation of this from the metaphysical point of view is quite different from what an ordinary person could imagine. No man on earth is capable of communicating with the angels in heaven, nor is an angel of heaven able to communicate with man.

But in the exceptional lives of the prophets, what happens is that they rise above all the planes which keep man removed from the angelic plane, and by doing so they are able to touch that angelic plane. And being charged with the ever-glowing fire of inspiration from the angelic spheres where they come in touch with angels, they descend to the plane of the earth. And it is then that their words become tongues of flame, as spoken of in the scriptures, which means every word of theirs becomes a torch in the hands of those who listen to illuminate their path through life. Especially in the lives of the great ones who have given a divine message, a religion to the world; their souls have never been disconnected in any form from the angelic world, and it is this current which has linked their souls with those of the angels, always keeping them in contact with heaven and the earth both. The soul of the prophet, therefore, is a link between heaven and the earth; it is a medium by which God's message can be received.

Then there are some pious souls who have the experience in their lives of having been warned or helped by an angel. It is such souls who have kept a thread unbroken, which they brought with them from the angelic world. They may be conscious of it or not, but there is a telegraphic wire which connects their souls with the souls of the angels, and they are conscious of having had contact with the angels.

Common disease is called normal health. When many cannot experience something which is rare, they think the person who experiences it has gone crazy. Therefore, it is the law of the mystics to see all things, to experience all things either of the earth or of heaven and yet say little, for the souls incapable of understanding the possibility of their reach will only mock at them.

There is another aspect of the contact with the angels, and that is at the time of death. Many have seen in their lives the angels of death, but at the time when death's call comes, some have seen them in a human form. Some have not seen them but heard them speak. The reason is that there are some souls who have already departed from the earth plane, though the breath is still there, connecting the soul with the body, and such souls experience, while still on earth, the angelic sphere at the time of their death. They see angels garbed in the form of their own imagination and hear their words in their own language. The reason is that it is necessary for a person who has lived on the earthly plane to clothe a being on the higher planes in earthly garments and to interpret immediately the language of the higher sphere in his own words.

For instance, the angel Gabriel spoke to Moses in the Hebrew language and to Muhammad in Arabic. One would ask, what was the language of Gabriel, Arabic or Hebrew? Neither Arabic nor Hebrew was the language of Gabriel. His language was the language of the soul, and the soul knows the language of the soul. When the soul interprets what it hears, even to itself, then it garbs the words in its own language.

There is a story in the Bible when the Spirit descended upon the twelve apostles and they began to speak all languages. The interpretation of the story is quite different. The meaning of this is that when the apostles were inspired by the angelic word, by that Divine Sun or the Holy Ghost, they knew the language of all languages, for it was the language of the soul, which means they heard man before man spoke to them; in other words, they were able to hear the voice of every soul on having that inspiration. It would not give credit to the apostles if one said they knew all the languages that are in the world instantly, for there are people just now to be found, whose genius in being linguists is so great that they happen to know more than thirty or forty languages, and even then they do not know all languages. There is only one language which may be called all languages and that is the language of the soul. Before the illuminated soul, all souls stand as written letters.

* * *

Question: *What is imagination, is it something unreal? Is there one angel of death?*

Answer: The imagination is everything. To the real all is real; to the unreal all is unreal.

Question: *Has it nothing to do with spiritual truth?*

Answer: Nothing.

Question: *What is it then?*

Answer: The angels are souls, purely.

31

The Soul Towards Manifestation

Question: *What part of the soul is it?*

Answer: It is not part of the soul; it is part of the mind. Imagination is the work of the mind.

Question: *Is there one angel of death?*

Answer: There is one and there are many. And yet in many there is one, and in one there are many.

Question: *Will you tell us something of the* asuras, *whose lives have been caught in the net of mortality?*

Answer: *Asura*s are those who have lost their souls. And the question is, how can one lose one's soul which is one's very life, and yet live? When I say they lost their soul, I do not mean to say that the soul left them, but that they lost consciousness of their soul. For the one who is not conscious of his soul, his spirit has lost it, at least from his consciousness. It is just like a person who buried a large sum of money in the ground on his farm. When he went to another country, somebody came and said, "All the money has been taken away," and this person became very unhappy. Now really speaking, that person did not tell the truth; the money was where it was buried. But just then the other was conscious of the loss, so for the moment he has lost it. When he will go and dig it up, he will find that it is there. But for the time, till he has dug it up, it is lost. So the soul is not lost in reality. But for the sake of convenience we say the soul is lost.

Question: *Why does the Roman Catholic Church divide the angels into nine grades? They say the seraphim are nearest to God, the archangels and angels are nearest to man?*

Answer: Variety always exists. Where there is a number of entities there will be variety; and in variety there will be a difference. And it is quite true; among human beings we find the same. Some are attracted to the earth, some to heaven, so among angels there is also the same tendency. One tendency is to be attracted to those who have gone further, which is man. Others are content being in heaven, in enjoying the heavenly bliss.

32

5

[Editor's Note: *The following questions and answers come from a Question and Answer class given before the next lecture. As in the other questions and answers, there is not a single theme, but since many of these questions and answers have some relation to the subject of the soul, the entire class is included here.*]

Question: *Will you please explain from a lesson on "shame": the sense of shame is like a pearl in a shell; the price cannot be given in the marketplace; the place of that pearl is the crown of the king?*[4]

Answer: That means that a virtue like this is appreciated and understood and rewarded fully in its right place. That is why it is said, "in the crown of the king." A person with this virtue is not appreciated by everybody. The person who has not got that virtue, he cannot appreciate it. Therefore, for a greater person, a greater place is required.

Question: *In the cases of obsession, does the body of the obsessed become really enfeebled?*

Answer: It depends upon the obsession. It might turn out otherwise if the obsession were different.

Question: *Can you tell me if a soul who has passed away young and who has been what we should call a pure soul on earth, does such a soul help more in a higher plane than he would on earth?*

Answer: Every soul inclined to help has a scope in every plane, on this plane as well as on the higher plane. The one who is able to help in this plane is able to help in the higher plane even more. And a pure soul can help here and in the higher plane even more.

Question: *Can you help somebody more as a human being or on a higher plane?*

Answer: In some ways and in some things you can help more as a human being, and in some other ways one can help more without a body. There are certain limitations of the human body. It cannot arrive in a certain place earlier than in due time. But once one has passed from this plane, one can reach it much sooner. The one who is living in the physical body has many more facilities also. Because when a person is face to face with his friend, he can help that friend much more than being hidden from the sight of the friend, who does not see him.

Question: *Do angels who come to experience life on the physical plane do so from choice, or is it predestined for them?*

Answer: This can only be answered if a person will read some of my writings on the subject of fate and free will, which are so interwoven. That which seems free will from one point of view is fate on the other, just the contrary. But at the same time, as the soul goes on, so it is building its destiny, it is making it. Therefore, fate and free will both are woven together. You cannot separate one from the other.

Question: *When one has the intention to do a thing, and a friend wants one not to do it, is it best to listen to one's own intuition or to follow the friend's advice?*

Answer: The answer depends upon which friend, whether a wise or a foolish friend, whether a true or a false friend, and what understanding that friend has, compared with one's own. Whether his intuition is greater than one's own. One cannot take it as a principle to always follow a person's advice. It might seem a virtue, but sometimes it will prove to be otherwise.

Question: *Can spiritual realization be attained in one moment, or must there always be a time of preparing?*

Answer: Yes, spiritual realization can be attained in one

moment in rare cases. But mostly a time of preparation is needed.

Question: *Will you give more particulars about the soul's journey when the body is asleep?*

Answer: Either the soul is caught in the mind during sleep, and it experiences the condition of the mind, or the soul enters into spiritual spheres, where it becomes charged with inspiration, power and a new life. And so when a person awakens, he feels more inspired, rested and invigorated, and very often blessed. A great load on his mind has been removed.

Question: *Does the soul sometimes have visits during the sleep of the body? Is it possible for a soul during the sleep of the body to visit another soul who [blank]? Is that in the power of the mind?*

Answer: It is the soul of the other person being reflected in the soul of this person. Then two persons have the same experience and the knowledge of the other's condition.

Question: *Is it possible for one of these souls to help the other?*

Answer: Yes, mostly one of those souls is advanced and has the power of help.

Question: *Do you consider the scientific or inventive genius to stand in the same relationship to the angelic sphere as prophetic genius?*

Answer: Yes, certainly. Although prophetic genius is all-embracing. But at the same time scientific or inventive genius also has the same source of inspiration, and all that depends upon inspiration has much to do with the angelic spheres.

Question: *Will you tell us if angels,* devas, *and nature spirits are different and if so in what way?*

Answer: Angels are the inhabitants of the angelic sphere. *Devas* are among men, such as *Wali, Ghous, Qutub, Nabi* and *Rasul*,[5] who although they have come on the earth as a fruit, having dropped on the earth, yet they are connected with the branch. The branch has bent and the fruit is touching the earth, but at the same time, it is still in [blank]; it has not yet lost the connection with the stem. It is that soul which is called *deva*. And the nature spirits, as human beings have souls, so also have the birds and beasts and insects. Not only the living creatures but also trees and plants, and planets and stars, everything that exists has a spirit at the back of it, and that spirit is its soul.

Question: *How can we know that it is the angel of death we see, if we clothe the angel with our imagination?*

Answer: But what is our imagination? Very often our imagination is inspiration, intuition. Especially at the time of death, a person is pitched to a very high state of being, and therefore, even a person who did not have much inspiration during his lifetime has it at that time when he is already lifted up closer to the higher sphere before the breath has left the body. And, therefore, though he garbs the angels with his imagination, still his intuition tells him that it is the angel of death.

Question: *Will you please tell us about guardian angels?*

Answer: Guardian angels are nothing but extra light on the path, one's own light and the light from above one is seeking. The person who holds himself closer to heaven, he has guidance from heaven; he is always guided. The one who disconnects himself from his original abode which is heaven, he then becomes worldly, earthly, just like a fruit which has broken from the tree and has fallen on the earth. But the one who still clings to the light of heaven, that person has still a light with him, about him, to guide him. And at every step that light comes, warns him, guides him, in accordance with his desire of being guided.

Question: *Can coming volcanic eruptions and earthquakes of nature be felt by sensitive people in advance? What is it that [blank]?*

Answer: Yes, there is an action and reaction: the action of nature upon people, and the action of people upon nature. That storm and wind have a certain effect upon us, on our word and speech [blank]. But this is also caused in some ways as a reaction to the conditions of the people. And, therefore, all wars and storms and floods and volcanic eruptions very often are caused by human beings, by the action or attitude or condition of humanity in general.

Question: *Sometimes in the old scriptures twin saviors are spoken about?*

Answer: I have not heard about it, but if I would give an interpretation, I would say the first twin saviors were Adam and Eve.

Question: *What did you say yesterday: "The Holy Ghost is the Divine Sun"? Is this the sun or the son?*[6]

Answer: I meant both.

6

THERE IS a phrase known to many, the guardian angel. This angel's protection comes to some souls on earth, such souls who are walking on the earth and yet are linked in some way or the other to the heavenly spheres. Often one sees an innocent child being saved from several accidents, and often a person is warned to save a child at the moment when the child is in danger. This guardian angel also appears in the same form as angels sent to people on different duties.

There are recording angels, who take a record of one's good actions and of bad actions. But the most interesting thing is that those who keep the record of good actions do not keep the record of bad actions; those who keep the record of bad actions are other angels. And there is a further explanation given by the Prophet on this subject, that often a discussion takes place between those who take the record of the good and the ones who take the record of man's bad things. The former do not believe in the latter, because they are only conscious of man's goodness. They cannot believe that one who is good can be bad also. Besides, those who record the good points want their record to be filled, and the other angels want their record to be filled, so there is a great rivalry between them.

Is this not the condition which we see in human nature? There is no person living on earth of whom all say good things and no one says bad things. So there is no person living about whom all say bad things and no one says any good. And the most interesting part for a keen observer of life is how each tries to prove his argument to be correct.

In Sufi terms these two are called the angels of *khair* and *khar*, and the difference is very little in their spelling: one is *khair* and the other is *khar*. That shows how little difference there is between goodness and badness. The ancient belief is that immediately after a person is buried, these two parties of angels come to his grave with their records and dispute about him. But do we not see in human nature the same thing? People do not even wait until after death; they begin to say good things and bad things about the person they know, about their friends and foes, and dispute over them.

There is also an ancient belief that after the dead person is in his grave and buried, there come two angels to ask him questions, and by this cross-examination prove their contrary arguments true. Their names are *munkir* and *nakir*; I think there is very little difference in their names. There is a story in the Bible[7] that Jacob wrestled with the angel all night and in the end, before the breaking of the morn, Jacob won. And the angel asked his name and blessed him. The interpretation of this is that the illuminated souls of the angels coming in contact with the earthly beings are in conflict, and that conflict ends when man has given up the earthly point of view and has adopted the heavenly point of view; then there is no more conflict, but a blessing. And the asking the name is a paradox: when once the false ego is crushed, the soul really does not know what his name is, for the name belongs to the false ego.

There is an old conception of nine kinds of angels; in reality there is one kind of angel, but their relation with human beings and their desire to experience life through human beings divides them into nine kinds. Then there is a belief that there are angels who are the inhabitants of heaven and others who live in the contrary place; those of heaven are called *nur*, and of the other place are called *nar*. This is an extreme point of view. In reality they can be distinguished as two kinds: *jelal* and *jemal*, the angels of power and the angels of beauty.

A question arises why the angels who descend onto earth as angels do not come as human beings, for every human being was originally an angel. The answer is that the angels who are related to human beings are human souls now in the angelic world who keep a connection with human beings because of their wish; and now that they have gone back from earthly regions to the angelic world, they still keep in touch with the earth, either being on a certain duty or because of their own pleasure.

* * *

Question: *Are the names of the angels, given by you, Arabic words?*

Answer: Yes, they are.

Question: *The great angels of whom we read in the scripture, such as Gabriel, were never in human life, were they?*

Answer: Gabriel is the chief angel of inspiration, of prophetic message, of revelation. And therefore, this is the central ray, the ray of the prophets, of the messengers, the inspirer of the great beings of the world; and therefore Gabriel is of his own kind.

Question: *Why are there nine kinds of angels?*

Answer: There are nine kinds because they are delighted in nine things.

Question: *Are the recording angels and the examining angels symbolical?*

Answer: Why symbolical, when their existence is a separate existence? They are angels. What is on the earth is in heaven. The nature and character of the earth is in heaven. If human nature has a tendency, in heaven they show the same tendency. And as men are concerned with the good and evil of one another, and so are angels.

Question: *Was it symbolical that they come to the grave and dispute over it?*

Answer: Yes, that is to some extent symbolical.

41

Question: *In any case they are no angels, for they do not live in the angelic sphere?*

Answer: You may call them no angels, but they are no human beings. You may call them by some other names, but they are angels just the same. Angels mean souls, and souls who have not been adorned with a human, earthly body and yet have come to experience life on the earth are still called angels. If they had had a human body, they would have been called human beings.

Question: *I thought they were not called angels, those who came back from earth, but spirits. Did you not say last time that angels had no contact with human beings?*

Answer: There are two kinds of angels: one is called *Malak*, the other *Farishta*. *Malak* is not in contact with human beings and comes not on the earth. But *Farishtas* are those human beings who have risen above spirits and have entered [blank] and have the liberty to experience earthly [blank]. It is the opposite of what they call *deva*, the one who has come on earth but yet is linked with heaven and always has the connection. So even with the angel who is still linked, the connection has not gone. Since I used the word angel only just now, I had to use for *Malik* and *Farishta* the word angel.

Question: *Do the angels who have descended on earth follow the lives of human souls and take real interest in their affairs, much the same as human souls do among them-selves?*

Answer: No, angels are not interested in the same way as human beings, because the kind changes and there is a great gap between them. Their interests are not the same. Therefore, if ever angels come onto the earth, either they are in touch with the innocent souls of children, because they are closer, or the interest is in the illuminated soul, the spiritual soul. Then they are interested in the being who is now passing away from the earth, going to their country.

The Soul Towards Manifestation

[Editor's Note: *Additional questions concerning this lecture, but asked on a separate occasion, are included here.*]

Question: *It seems to me that the recording angels support the theory of karma.*

Answer: Yes, someone must support it.

Question: *As the recording angels write down the good and the bad actions there must be a judge, for who would tell them what is good and what is bad?*

Answer: The judge lies in man's heart. It is from man's heart that the angels read what they have to notice as his good and as his bad actions.

7

THE ANGELIC spheres, the highest heavens, are the spheres of light called *nur*; and that current of power, which runs through the divine sun, causes rays to spread, each ray being an angel or a soul. It is this divine current which, really speaking, is *nafs*, which means breath or the ego. Breath is the ego, and ego is the breath. When the breath has left the body, the ego has gone. The nature of this current, which spreads as a ray and which is a life-current, is to collect and to create. It collects the atoms of the sphere in which it is running, and it creates out of itself all that it can create. Therefore, in the angelic sphere, which is the sphere of radiance, the soul collects the atoms of radiance.

A Sufi poet of Persia has given a most beautiful expression of this idea in a verse. He says: "A glow garbed with a flame came." No better picture of an angel can one make than this. Before the angels were drawn by artists in the form of human beings, they were symbolized as burning lamps; from this comes the custom of lighting candles in religious services, showing thereby to some extent what the angels were like before they became human souls.

In the scriptures it is mentioned that human beings by their virtues produced angels; this is only a symbolical expression. It is not that human beings produced angels by their virtues, but their virtues lifted their souls to find angels or connect them with the angels.

One may ask, "If the souls who have settled in the angelic world are angels, then what makes them come to the earth? How can they experience life on the earth?" The answer is that it is not the angels who have settled who come to the earth. The reason is that they have finished their creative power in manifesting as angels. If they had a greater power, they certainly would have gone further into the physical spheres and would have manifested as human beings, for the desire of every soul is to reach culmination in manifestation, and that culmination is a stage of the human plane.

For the souls who return from the earth, it is their part to communicate with the earth very often, and it is such angels who are known to man. If the angels who have never manifested as man on earth ever experience life on the earth, it is only through the medium of the minds and bodies of those who by their evolution come closer to the angelic spheres. They take these as their instruments and at times reflect themselves in them and at times have them be reflected in themselves.

* * *

Question: *If* nafs *exists as far back as the angelic plane, how can human beings hope to get free from it?*

Answer: Human beings do not need to get free from it. Only they need to distinguish between true *nafs* and false.

Question: *Is the nafs the word you give to the false ego?*

Answer: Yes, it is; it is ego.

Question: *How long did Prophet Muhammad's mission last? What age was he when he died?*

Answer: I think sixty, I am not sure. His mission lasted for about twenty years.[8]

Question: *When angels experience life on the earth through the medium of the mind and body of human beings, is this obsession and must it be avoided?*

Answer: Certainly, it is obsession, but in the case of an angel, it could better be named inspiration. But at the same time, in the case of an angel, it is not necessary to avoid it. Because from there one gets nothing but light. All inspiration comes from the angelic spheres.

46

Question: *One would be very fortunate to get it, no?*

Answer: Yes, I should think so.

Question: *Are there any distinctions or differences of race, nationality or religion between the souls who have passed from the physical plane?*

Answer: The differences and distinctions remain still. It is not so very easy to get rid of them. Wherever there is a world of variety, there are differences. Yes, one can say that in the higher plane there are less distinctions; in the lower plane there are more. Even among human beings we find the more evolved, the less distinctions, and the less evolved, the more distinctions.

Question: *Do you mean that angels who have not manifested obsess human beings?*

Answer: Yes, it is so.

Question: *Could you use a more beautiful word, because obsession is always connected with less good things; perhaps inspired?*

Answer: Yes, inspired. When the force emanates from the divine source it projects rays going towards manifestation.

Question: *Does each ray spread in all directions?*

Answer: Yes. The nature of the rays is the same in the divine spheres as in the physical sphere. We see this by studying the rays of the sun.

Question: *How do you account for the fact that the soul is centered in the particular point where the physical body is, where the person is experiencing life in the physical body?*

Answer: It is in the body in one way. It functions in the body, although the soul is incomparably larger than the body. Just a little point of the soul itself functions in the body. For the impression that one has is of the soul being centered in the body, when, as a matter of fact, it extends throughout the universe.

Question: *Are the angels you spoke of in your third lecture, who live on the earth, not the* jinns?

Answer: No. I have not yet come as far as the world of *jinns*.

Question: *Do the angels of the angelic sphere also experience birth and death, youth and old age?*

Answer: Not in the sense that we are accustomed to understand. But at the same time there is only one being, which is God, who is above birth and death. But all of manifestation, from the point of duality to the myriads of beings, are all subject to the law of birth and death. Only, the difference between birth and death is very great between the plane of human beings and the planes of angels. And at the same time there is the youth and age of each thing we see, of the plant and fruit; there is a time when they are raw and a time when they are ripe. So it is with the angels, but there is no comparison of the life of angels to the life of human beings. Human life is too limited compared to the life of angels. Even the birth of a thought or idea is incomparably small compared to the life of angels.

Question: *As man is judged by the God in his own heart, I do not understand what the use is of this outside recording of our actions?*

Answer: But it all goes on in the plane of our life, even of the angels. We are accustomed to put it outside, but it all is in our heart, and therefore, it is not outside at all; it is in the heart.

The heart is a mirror which has two sides. It reflects all that is outside and all that is within. And therefore, God, and angels, and all that is within is reflected in the heart, and all that is outside is also reflected, because it has two sides. It is not necessarily a piece of flesh. The heart of flesh is only that part of the body which was made first, and upon which the whole body was formed. And therefore, as it was made first, it is more sensitive to the heart which is within than any other organ. And therefore, when there is a depression or joy or pleasure, every little excitement or little feeling has a feeling in the heart. Because man does not see the heart which is the mirror, but feels it in the heart, even that piece of flesh which one calls the heart is the seat of the function, though the soul is incomparably greater than the body. But the body is the seat of it. Therefore, man gives a great importance to his body.

Question: *Can every atom of manifestation be said to have a soul?*

Answer: Certainly, because manifestation has begun, has commenced from the heavenly source, from the divine spheres, and therefore every atom of this universe, mental or material, is an outcome of that. And therefore, it cannot exist without a part of that heavenly radiance with it. Even an atom of dust has behind it a radiance. And if it were not for this radiance, it would not have manifested to our view. We see it because it has light in it. It is its own light that shows it to us; that is its soul.

What seems to be void of intelligence is not in reality void of it; only, intelligence is buried in its heart. It is, so to speak, that intelligence has projected itself, and then its own outcome has covered it, and buried intelligence in itself. But the intelligence must come out someday. Therefore, through all these phases of life, it is trying to break out. You can see this in volcanic eruptions, this power working through floods, lightning, planets, stars. Its desire is to burst out of where it is, in a way, captive, and its chance of raising itself is in human life. And therefore spirituality is the only object in the fulfillment of human evolution.

Question: *Is that what is sometimes meant in the phrase, the spiritual realization of matter?*

Answer: Yes.

8

SOULS in the angelic spheres live as a breath. The soul in its nature is a current, a current, the nature of which is to envelop in itself all that might come along and meet it on its way. The soul collects all that comes to it; therefore, it becomes different from its original condition. Yet in its real being the soul is a vibration, the soul is a breath, the soul is the essence, the soul is intelligence and the soul is the essence of personality.

The question very often arises: "If an angel comes from above, does it descend outwardly before a person or within a person, in his heart?" This question may be answered that the lift for the soul is situated within, not without, which brings the soul down to earth and takes it back towards heaven. That lift is the breath. The soul comes with the breath to earth, and with the same it returns.

Those among human beings who are not even aware of their own breath, how can they know who came within and who went away? Many seem wide awake to the life without but asleep within. And though the chamber of the heart is continually visited by the hosts of heaven, they do not know their heart, they are not there.

There is a very interesting story told in the Arabic scriptures, that God made Iblis the chief among all the angels and then told him to bring some clay that God might make out of it an image. The angels under the direction of Iblis brought the clay and made an image. Then God breathed into that image and asked the angels to bow before him. All the angels bowed, but Iblis. He said, "Lord, thou hast made me the chief of all angels, and I have brought the clay at thy command and made with my own hands this image, which thou commandest me to bow before." The displeasure of God arose and fell on his neck as the sign of the outcast.

It is by that story that we learn what Jesus Christ has said in the Bible[9]: "Blessed are the meek, who will inherit the kingdom of the earth." What Iblis denied was the reflection of God in man; and that law one can observe in everything in life. A person may be rich with wealth or high in position, but he must listen to the policeman, for it is not the rank or wealth which the policeman has, but in him is reflected the power of the mighty government and when one takes no heed of what the policeman says, one refuses to obey the law of the state. In everything, small or big, it is the same law. And in every person there is a spark of the Iblis tendency, the tendency which we know as egotism, the tendency of saying: "No, I will not listen, I will not give in, I will not consider." Because of what? Because of "I," because of "I am."

But there is only one "I," the perfect "I," who is God, whose power is mightier than any power existing in the world, whose position is greater than any one. And he shows it in answer to that egoistic tendency of man, who is limited. This is expressed in that English saying: "Man proposes but God disposes." It is this idea which teaches man the virtue of resignation, which shows man that the "I" that he claims is a much smaller "I," and there is no comparison between his "I" and the "I" of the great ego, God.

And there is another story, the story which tells how frightened the soul was when it was commanded to enter the body of clay. It was most unwilling, not from pride but from fear. The soul whose nature is freedom, whose dwelling is the heavens, whose comfort is to be free to dwell in all the spheres of existence—for that soul to go and sit in a house made of clay was most horrifying. Then God asked the angels to play and sing, and the ecstasy that was produced in the soul by hearing the singing made it enter into that body of clay, where it was captive to death.

Now, the interpretation of this idea is that the soul, which is pure intelligence and angelic in its being, had not the least interest in dwelling in the physical spheres, which rob it of its freedom and make it limited. But what interested the soul and made it come into the body is what this physical world offers to the senses, which produces such an intoxication that it takes away the thought of the heavens for the moment from the soul, and so it becomes captive in the physical body.

What is Cupid? Is not Cupid the soul? It is the soul, it is the angel, the angel going towards manifestation, the angel who has arrived at his destiny, which is the human plane; before it has manifested as such, it is Cupid.

* * *

Question: *You said that enjoyment through the senses made the soul willing to remain in the body. Does it get more enjoyment from the senses on earth than it would without them in heaven?*

Answer: No, I did not say that the enjoyment of the senses made the soul willing to remain in the body. I have said that the enjoyment through the senses made the soul come into the body. It would not have entered otherwise. Because through the senses the physical life became intelligible to the soul, and therefore, this intoxicated the soul so that it entered the body. But there is one question: Before entering the body, how did it experience the senses? First it experienced the senses through the senses of other mediums, those who are in the body. As the child shares the food of the mother before birth, so it experiences through the senses before its own senses have developed.

Question: *Then the desire is to have for itself [question incomplete].*

Answer: Yes.

Question: *Does it get more enjoyment by the senses on earth than it would without them in heaven?*

53

Answer: Certainly. Because the enjoyment that the soul gets here on earth by the medium of the senses is just like wine touched to the lips. It is an illusion, it is no wine. As the world is illusive, so enjoyment is the same. It has never made one happy, nor will it ever make one happy forever. The pleasure of the world comes and goes; for the moment it is pleasant, afterwards it is nothing. There is only one pleasure which is real happiness. It does not belong to earth. If the person who is living on the earth is happy, he is not happy with earthly things, only with the realization of heaven, when he connects his soul with the heavenly spheres. But in the things of the earth there is no happiness, except the pleasure which is illusive.

Question: [*question not recorded*]

Answer: A soul which is in the body, although connected with heaven, is still open to the influences of the earth. Not only open, but dependent for its external life on the food of the earth and the water. As its life depends upon the things of the earth, it still seeks for the pleasures of the earth. The closer to heaven a person is drawn, the less important the pleasures of the earth become. All that seems to be pleasure fades away; it has no color, no taste any more. Therefore, the religions have taught self-denial by denying all the pleasures of the earth. But I think a soul which naturally rises towards heaven does not need to practice self-denial. It comes by itself as the soul grows and rises towards heaven.

Question: *Was not that the question of a soul who had not yet manifested? Why should a soul leave the greater happiness of heaven, which is so much greater, for earthly pleasures?*

Answer: The idea is that the tendency of every motive is to go to the utmost point, the farthest point, whether in its result it gives happiness or unhappiness. The tendency of the one who has every motive [every intent] will experience it to its final result. For instance, a singer sings. He sings very comfortably on the lower note. His heart's desire is to go as high as he can go. He may take a chance of breaking his voice, but his tendency is to go to the highest note. It is the same tendency when people crave to go to the North Pole. If their life were taken away, or whatever suffering, they will go to the extreme end of the world.

If there were not that tendency, there would not have been this manifestation. Even at the cost of all the happiness the soul touches [blank]. Human evolution comes to that great fulfillment which even angels are not blessed with. Therefore, there is an advantage in every loss. There is a loss for the time being, but there is a greater benefit in the end.

Question: *This includes the lower kingdom near every stage of the [blank]?*

Answer: Yes.

Question: *A human being who goes home is further than an angel who never comes on earth?*

Answer: Yes.

Question: *The soul, as a part of the whole consciousness, carries with it the same tendency which God has, to see himself in his manifestation?*

Answer: Yes.

Question: *What does the sign of the outcast mean, which that angel received?*

Answer: I have interpreted it as the sign of the outcast. In Sanskrit the word is *tok*; it means the same, that something was taken away from him which made him chief, which was the secret of evolution, of progress. But plainly speaking, the soul who has not yet realized the almighty power of God, and the perfect wisdom of God, and has not compared its own limited power and wisdom with the almighty power and wisdom of God, is in the same place where Iblis was. Every soul to some extent is [blank]. But the moment the soul compares its own limitation to the perfection of God, it is already on the way of progress, because it realizes. And becoming conscious of one's imperfection gives one the tendency to go forward.

55

Question: *Is fear inherent in the soul? When it fears being born in the human being, does it also fear before death?*

Answer: Fear is a shadow cast upon the light of the soul. And of what is that shadow? That shadow is of something that the soul does not know, something that is strange to the soul. For instance, take a person who has never learned to swim near the water; he is not acquainted with the water, he is not at ease there. There is his fear. Another person gets rid of that strange feeling, knows his own power over the water; he has no more fear. Therefore, fear comes from ignorance. As everyone fears to go into the dark room as he does not know what is there, so the soul in entering the body of clay naturally is frightened.

Question: *In death is it the fear of the soul or of the body, of the physical body to be broken up?*

Answer: The soul does not know what death is, that is the strangeness. When one has become acquainted with death [blank].

Question: *If a person is obsessed to write automatically in a normal state of mind or in a trance, shall he do so, or resist this tendency? Even if it seems inspired by an enlightened guiding spirit? If he is to follow the call, how can he tell if it comes from a good or evil power?*

Answer: The soul must not take upon itself such a risk of attempting anything in the line of phenomena, because it is full of danger for a soul unacquainted with such things. And if they ever want to have any experience in that way, they must first of all find a teacher in whom they have full trust, and then ask him if they are fit for it.

9

THE SOUL which has passed through the angelic plane comes into the plane of the *jinn*. It is the plane of the mind, and this plane may be called the spiritual plane for it is mind and soul which make spirit. The souls who halt in this plane, being attracted to the beauty of this plane, settle here. Also the souls who have no more power to go farther into outer manifestation become the inhabitants of this plane. Therefore, there are three kinds of souls who meet on this plane on their way to manifestation: the souls who are attracted to this plane and who decide to remain here; the souls who are unable to go further and have to be settled in this plane; and the souls who are continuing their journey towards the earthly plane and are on their way to the earth through this plane.

The *jinn* is an entity with mind but not such a mind as that of man, but a mind more pure, more clear, which is illuminated by the light of intelligence. The mind of the *jinn* is deeper in perception and in conception because it is empty, not filled up with thoughts and imaginations as that of man. It is the mind of the *jinn* which may be called the empty cup, a cup into which knowledge can be poured out, in which there is an accommodation.

It is for this reason that the teachers on the spiritual path appreciate the *jinn* quality in the minds of their pupils, in which they find accommodation for knowledge. A cup which is already filled, or even somewhat filled, does not give free accommodation to that knowledge which the teacher wishes to pour out into the heart of his pupil. As the *jinn* is keen in perception and conception, so it is keen in

57

expression, either through word or deed. The action of the *jinn* extends as far as the mind can reach. The word of the *jinn* reaches much further than the voice, for it takes as its route the mental sphere which is above the air waves.

The *jinn* comes closer to man than an angel for in the *jinn* there is something like the mind, which of course is complete in man. All the intuitive and inspirational properties are possessed by the *jinn* because that is the only source that the *jinn* has of receiving its knowledge. Subjects such as poetry, music, art, inventive science, philosophy and morals are akin to the nature of the *jinn*. The artist, therefore, and the poet, the musician and the philosopher show in their gift the *jinn*-heritage, which proves them through life to be geniuses.

The word *jinn* comes from a Sanskrit word *jnanan*, meaning knowledge. *Jinns*, therefore, are beings of knowledge, whose hunger is for knowledge, whose joy is in learning, in understanding, and whose work is inspiring and bringing joy and light to others. In every kind of knowledge that exists, the most favorite knowledge to a *jinn* is the knowledge of truth, in which is the fulfillment of its life's purpose.

* * *

Question: *Can the light of the soul be so great that it illuminates the room in darkness? I know a child who always saw clearly in a perfectly dark room. What is it?*

Answer: Certainly, the illuminated soul finds its way through the darkness within and without, both.

Question: *Is the aura part of the soul, or the soul itself, or what is it?*

Answer: It is the reflection of the soul in an ethereal plane.

Question: *Are there good and bad jinns?*

Answer: Where there is good, there is bad. Good cannot exist without bad. If *jinns* are good, so *jinns* must be bad also.

Question: *Are there good and bad angels?*

Answer: If there are good angels, then there are bad also. The question is only if they are good. They cannot be good if there were no bad. They can only be good on the condition that some of them are bad.

Question: *Would you tell us if souls remain a very long time on the angelic and jinn planes on the return journey, as they do on the way to manifestation?*

Answer: Yes, certainly. Free will is the basis of the whole life. In spite of all limitations and helplessness that man meets through life there is a wonderful power in man's soul if it were discovered. What makes man helpless is the ignorance of the power of free will in him. It is God-power. Therefore, it is a most wonderful power. It is the ignorance of this which keeps man in darkness in regard to his divine heritage. And every difficulty he meets with through life, owing to life's limitations, covers that divine spark of free will which is in him, and in time it becomes obscure to his view, which culminates in the tragedy of life.

Question: *What is meant by the age of Aquarius?*

Answer: That is a new word to me.

Question: *A book is called* The Age of Aquarius. *It is what we have to expect.*

Answer: I really do not know. I know what we expect, but I do not know what he expects.

Question: *Can these* jinn *souls also attain mastery, or through one of the other paths reach spiritual attainment?*

Answer: Yes, they all do. Some do more than the others. But as I have said, and I shall repeat it a thousand times: Not only the souls of the angels, *jinns* and human beings, but even the animals and birds, trees and plants, and the smallest germ and insect, they all have a spiritual fulfillment in their life. And if that would not have been in their life, the life would have been a waste. No creature that has ever

59

been born on earth will be deprived of that spiritual bliss, however bad or wrong that person may seem to be. It is only a matter of time, and a difference of process, through which one has to touch it.

As I have said, that as human beings with their different plane of evolution will have a moment, a day, when they will touch that spiritual bliss, so even the animals, carnivorous or herbivorous, birds or insects, all have a moment, a moment of promise. And that promise is the fulfillment of the promise of their life. Even if an insect has been born for one moment, the purpose of that moment has been accomplished.

And by this we understand that there is nothing in this world which is here without a purpose. And by this we learn that although our place in the scheme of life and our work in this plan of the whole universe may seem different, one from the other, yet in the sum total of things we all, as the lower creation, together with the *jinns* and angels, have one and the same result, and that result is the realization of truth, in greater or smaller degree, which comes to all in the form of bliss.

Question: *Is it true that animals have a group soul, not each a soul?*

Answer: That is a conception of some people, but there is one and there are many. These two things must be understood. In manifestation there are many; in truth there is one. In fact there are many; in truth there is one. For instance, there is a rise and fall of a nation; and there is a prosperity and declining of a race; and so there is also the birth and death of a world. But at the same time with all these group souls we all are individual entities, and so with the animals. And at the same time we are one; we become one as a race, as the whole world. In this sense, if a person wants to make a speculation about the animals having a group soul, he may. But in point of fact, every animal, tree, plant has its own soul and spirit. They may call it by a different name. One might see in the form of a group soul, as France as a nation has its good or bad [blank]. That is another thing.

If we admit that the animals have a group soul, then we must admit that human beings have a group soul also. Neither by speculating on that do we produce a new doctrine or theory, nor by not admitting it do we show a greater wisdom. Both are right. We can be a group and we can be one. As our body is a group, and yet every part is a separate thing. If the hand is hurt, one separate thing has been hurt. If we go into this matter more deeply, we shall find a most wonderful phenomenon working through life and we shall come to a place where the whole being shall unveil itself, and we shall be able to see nothing but God.

Question: *Can a soul after death see conditions which were hidden from it during earthly life?*

Answer: Certainly. Death is the opening of a cover, after which there are many things which will be known to the soul, which have been so far hidden from it, in regard to its own life and in regard to the whole world.

10

THE *JINN* WORLD is a world of minds. It may be called a mental world and yet the soul is with the mind. The soul with the mind is called spirit, and, therefore, it may be called a spiritual world. The questions what the *jinns* are like, and what they look like, I will answer in the same way as I have in explaining the forms of angels. Things are not always as they are, but also as we see them. Man always pictures the beings he imagines and cannot see with his physical eyes as something like himself. Or man's imagination may gather different forms, for instance wings from the birds, and horns, and paws from tigers. He puts them all together and makes a new form. It is beyond possibility to explain exactly how a *jinn* looks, and yet there is no existing being who lives without form.

In support of man's imagination, which pictures angels or *jinns* more or less in the form of man, there is much that can be said. For everything in the world proves at the end of examination that it is striving to culminate into the form of man. The rocks and trees, fruits and flowers, mountains and clouds, all show themselves to be developing gradually towards the image of man. A keen observer of nature will prove this a thousand times. There is everything in the world to support this argument: how every form shows either a part of human form or an undeveloped outline. As it is with material things, so it is with the lower creation, and in the same way it is towards the human form that the angel and the *jinn* are growing. It is this idea which is spoken in the scriptures: "We have created man in our own image." If I were to add a word of explanation, I would say: "To make the image of man, we have made all forms."

The world of *jinns* is the world of minds, yet the minds of *jinns* are not so developed as the minds of men. The reason is that the experience of life on the earth completes the making of the mind. In the *jinn* world, the mind is only a design, an outline, a design which is not yet embroidered. To the questions what is the occupation of *jinns*, and what does the world of *jinns* looks like, one may give a thousand explanations, but nothing will explain it fully. For instance, if a person would ask me what China looks like, I would tell him: "It is most wonderful, most interesting." But if they ask: "What is wonderful and interesting?" I would say: "Go and take a trip to China in order to see it fully."

We have not sufficient words to explain what a *jinn* is like or what the world of the *jinn* is. But what little can be said about it is that it is a world of music, a world of art, of poetry, a world of intelligence, cheerfulness and joy, a world of thought, imagination and sentiment, a world that a poet would approve of, and a musician would crave to experience.

The life of the *jinn* is the ideal life for a thinker to be in, a life which is free from all illnesses, pure from all the bitterness of human nature, free to move about without any hindrance through space, and most joyful. There the sun of intelligence shines, the trouble of birth and death is not so severe, and life not so short as on the earth. If there is any paradise, it is the world of *jinns*. Hindus have called it *Indra loka* and pictured *gandharva*s and *apsara*s to be there, a paradise which every prophet has spoken of to his followers in the way that they could understand.

The question, how does a prophet know, may be answered by saying that the soul of the prophet is like a fruit, which by its weight is touching the ground; it has not dropped onto the earth, it is still connected with the branch to which it is attached, the branch which comes through all planes. Therefore, he, in his experiences, so to speak, touches different worlds. And it is in this mystery which is hidden prophetic genius and prophetic inspiration. It is through this current that the fruit is connected with the stem. Therefore, though on the earth, the prophet speaks of the heavens, though on the earth, he calls aloud the name of God. To many God is an imagination, to him God is a reality.

* * *

Question: *What do* jinn*s look like to each other? What do human beings look like to* jinn*s? What do angels look like to* jinn*s?*

Answer: That the *jinn* must answer.

Question: *Do angels inspire men as well as the* jinn*s?*

Answer: Certainly, they both inspire men.

Question: *Are* jinn*s sent to the earth with messages, like the angels?*

Answer: Certainly they are.

Question: *Do the* jinn*s know their own imagination as imagination or as external things?*

Answer: The ego is at the back of everything. Their mind is more capable of knowing. They have more innocence and less wisdom.

Question: *Should people live longer than they do if conditions were better?*

Answer: There have been times when man lived much longer than now. Life is not meant to be painful, and yet in human life one experiences pain in everything, pain in birth and in death. It should not be. It comes from the artificial life, from an unnatural state of living; man has gone far beyond the normal state of living.

Question: *Do* jinn*s communicate with spirits returned from experiencing the earth?*

Answer: Yes, sometimes they do communicate, but they are much happier in their own surroundings. They do not like it, it destroys their knowledge and their peace, it is not agreeable to them. For instance, the inhabitants of a certain country, who are pure from the knowledge of other countries, are much happier in their own country and in their own way. But if some go out and bring knowledge of other countries, it is not agreeable to them. And the same way with the *jinn*.

Question: *What is meant by the Greek saying, "Those the gods love, die young"?*

Answer: It is an exaggeration; saying it only means that even in the death of young people there is the love of God; there is something better for them, which those on this side do not know.

11

[Editor's Note: *The following questions and answers come from a brief question and answer period, probably given before the following lecture. As in the other questions and answers, there is not a single theme, but since many of these questions and answers have some relation to the subject of the soul, the entire class is included here.*]

Question: *What is an elemental?*

Answer: Just as there are the beings of water and earth, who live in the water and live on the earth, so there are the beings who live in the elements, in the air and [blank]. It is such beings who are called elementals. The visible things we do not call elementals, only those who have no physical body.

Question: *What do you mean by the feeling of dizziness one feels standing on a height?*

Answer: The cause of it is expressive of a very great secret, the secret why there are many people who are afraid of the spiritual truth. They would like to run away from the place where spiritual truth is spoken. I do not mean that they do not like the Church or God mentioned before them, but if you tell them some secret of God, they want to run away. They get the same feeling as a person who stands on the top of the mountain and looks below. Because they see such a gulf before them, they are afraid because they feel attraction.

Why does the dizziness come? Because the earth attracts one. It is quite possible that that attraction would become so great that they would be without control or resistance and would jump down. Because it is a kind of magnet which is attracting them with power. A man holds himself back from it, with force, not to jump. Wherever there is a gap and there is an attraction, there is that feeling.

I have very often met people who, as soon as the philosophical ideas began, and the relation between God and man, that person gets so afraid there comes that feeling of dizziness: because he cannot deny the truth of it, but he wants to save his life from the attraction. It is the fear of a gap, of a wide horizon which a person is not accustomed to see. But it is a matter of getting accustomed. There are builders of houses, who stand on the highest top of the house, especially in America; there they are working and from there look down and move about. They do not fear; they have become accustomed.

It is exactly the same with the sage, the thinkers. The picture of the workers on the high houses is the same picture of the sage who looks at what may be called the life on the surface and the eternal life. What people call death becomes a bridge for him. The more he thinks of it, the less fear he has. There is a saying of a Sufi: "The *wali*[10] has no fear of death;" he loses the fear of death.

Question: *Is the color of flame red or yellow?*

Answer: Flame is not heat. It is the glow which is heat. Flame is only a light. The real heat is in the glow. If one catches the glow, the hand burns, not if one touches the flame. In other words, one may say: the red fire covered by yellow.

Question: *And the blue in the flame?*

Answer: Blue is the breath in the flame. The day when science will discover the secret of electricity fully, on that day science will also discover the secret of the soul. Because the secret of the soul is not very far from the secret of electricity. For instance, let earth help: What [blank] the current of electricity and what forms into flame is not necessarily electricity. Electricity is that power which is hidden there, in the current, not that which is manifest. If that is understood, then the explanation of the soul will be the same.

The body is composed of the atoms by which the body

exists in the physical world—physical atoms attracted by some secret current. That secret current is the soul. In one globe, there is another globe. There is something within the body, but at the same time it is all collected and gathered by that current which is within. That current is the soul, the ray of the divine sun. And one can also understand that this current in the heavenly spheres, in the angelic sphere, attracts angelic atoms, heavenly atoms. In another sphere, it attracts other atoms. In the physical sphere it attracts physical atoms. Therefore, mankind is already dressed in the angelic dress; over the dress of the *jinn* he has put the dress of the human being. He really has all three dresses, one over the other.

Question: *When you speak to [question incomplete]?*

Answer: In interest there is a very high blessing. When the first [blank]. The story in *Arabian Nights* [blank]. There was a wall that was called a wall of mystery.[11] Many people used to [blank].

Question: *From where does the fear of death come?*

Answer: Ignorance of the self gives the fear of death. The more one learns from the self, the less fear of death there is. The more one lives in one's soul, the less hold one has upon the body. The body has fear according to the consciousness it has in itself.

Man is not only dependent upon his mind for thought, but every atom of the body is to some extent conscious, and it protects itself. Man must learn to control his consciousness and then he can raise it. When a person is conscious of a headache, he feels the headache, but when asleep, then he is not conscious of the headache and does not feel it. If a person could collect his consciousness automatically and raise it step by step by the power of will, he would rise above pain. The degree of consciousness in the atoms is dependent upon the soul.

12

THE SOUL is a current—call it electric. Unlike the electric current which we know on this physical plane, different from this in its power and influence, it is a current which runs more speedily than anything we know, a current which is beyond time and space, a current which runs through all the planes of life.

If manifestation is the breath of God, souls are breaths of God. According to the Yogi's conception, there is one breath and there are many breaths. The one breath, which is the central breath, is called by the Yogis *prana*, and every other breath which has a certain part to play in the mechanism of the human body, all such breaths are called breaths. And again, *prana* and all other breaths, when put together, make one breath which we call life. The souls, therefore, are different breaths of God and all the different breaths put together make one breath, the divine breath, which is life.

The elements of every sphere are different, just as the air of every part of the world is different, the water is different, its effect upon the human being is different. So the atoms of every plane are different. Their nature and character are as different as their effect. Therefore, the form of the angel need not be compared in any way with the form of the *jinn*; neither can the form of the *jinn* be compared with the form of man, for the atoms with which the *jinn* is made belong to another sphere.

A man who is accustomed to physical forms cannot very well grasp the idea of the forms of the *jinn*s. This shows us that the soul shoots itself forth and functions in a body which that particular sphere offers. The heavens, for instance, offer that luminous body to the soul which in Sufi terms is called *nur*, because heaven is made of luminous atoms—it is all illumination. It is the recognition of that angelic body in the Buddha which made his disciples make the statue of Buddha in gold. Often artists have the conception of an angel to be painted in gold, for it represents light.

The soul that goes as far as the sphere of the *jinn*, as a current coming from the heavens, functions in a body of the *jinn* world.

The question is: But a soul which comes from the heavens, from the world of angels, does it come to the *jinn* world without a body? The answer is: No, it comes with a body, an angelic body, yet it becomes necessary for the soul coming with the angelic body into the jinn world to be adorned with a body of that particular world in order to stand the weather of that plane. The animals which live in cold countries have a different skin from those that live in tropical countries. That is the condition for going into any other sphere. Even if a person were journeying, going from one tropical country to another, if on the way he has to pass through a climate which is cold, he will need suitable garments for that climate. What is the body? The body is a garment of the soul. The soul wears this garment in order to stand the weather of that particular sphere.

The souls who are passing through the *jinn* sphere towards the physical plane, and who do not stop in the *jinn* plane, meet with the travellers on their journey back home. They learn from them a great many things. There is a give and take, there is buying and selling, there is learning and teaching; but who teaches the most? The one with more experience, the one who is [going] back home. This gives the map of the journey to the soul travelling towards manifestation. It is from that map that the travelling soul strikes his path, rightly or wrongly.

A soul may have one instruction; another soul may have more instruction. One may be clear; another may be puzzled. Yet they all go forward as the travellers of a caravan, taking with them all the precious information and things they have learned from the others. It is, therefore, that every child born on earth, besides what he has inherited from his parents and ancestors, possesses a power and knowledge quite peculiar to himself, different from what his parents or ancestors possessed. Yet he knows not where he received it, nor who gave him that knowledge, but he shows from the beginning of his life on earth signs of having known things which have never been taught to him.

One soul is more impressionable than another soul; one soul is perhaps more impressed by the angelic plane and that impression has remained deeper in that soul throughout the whole journey. There is another soul who is more impressed by the *jinn* world, and that impression lasts with that soul all through the journey. There is another soul who has not gotten that impression from the angelic world or from the *jinn* world. That soul does not know either of heaven or of the *jinn* plane; what it knows is from the earth, and it is only interested in the things of the earth. One generally finds among artists, poets, musicians, thinkers, writers and philosophers, also among inventors, administrators, and great politicians, *jinn* souls who have brought with them to earth some deep impression which proves them in their lives to be great geniuses.

Impression is a great phenomenon itself. Man is as he thinketh, and what is it that man thinks? He thinks of that in which he is most interested. And what he is most interested in, that he himself is. Do we not see in our life on earth some people, deeply impressed with a certain personality, ideal, thought or feeling, having become the same in time? If that is true, what is man? Man is his impression. The soul, impressed deeply in the *jinn* world by some personality coming back from the earth, an impression deeply engraved upon that soul which the soul can never throw away, certainly becomes itself that personality with which it was impressed.

Suppose a soul impressed in the *jinn* world with the personality of Beethoven, when born on earth is Beethoven in thought, in feeling, in tendency, in inclination, in

73

knowledge; only in addition to that personality he has the heritage of his parents and of his ancestors. As the son of a certain family is called by the name of the same family, so the impression of a certain personality may rightfully be called by the name of the same personality. Therefore, if Shankaracharya[12] claimed to be the reincarnation of Krishna, there is every reason for his claim, as this theory stands in support of this.

Life from beginning to end is a mystery. The deeper one dives in order to investigate the truth, the more difficulty one finds in distinguishing what is called personality. But it is not the aim of the wise to distinguish personality; their wisdom is in the understanding of the secret of personality, its composition and its decomposition, which resolves in the end in the one personality. "There is one God; none exists save he."[13]

* * *

Question: *Are there other worlds besides the angelic and the jinn world that impress the souls who are going towards manifestation?*

Answer: No, only these two worlds.

Question: *Do witches and vampires develop their power by intuition? From where do they get their knowledge? Where have their souls been impressed by this tendency, going towards manifestation?*

Answer: Sometimes; but sometimes they have learned these traits after coming on the earth. Mostly the bad traits belong on the earth.

Question: *Is it not an impure intuition?*

Answer: No, intuition is never impure.

Question: *An instinct?*

Answer: No. Impurity belongs to the earth. Intuition is a heavenly bliss.

Question: *Does it happen that there is a tendency in a family to be* jinn *persons?*

Answer: Like attracts like.

Question: *If a soul meets Beethoven in the angelic world, and another soul meets Beethoven in the* jinn *world, is the impression different and is the result in these souls' life on earth different?*

Answer: Yes, they will be different. For after manifestation one will show the soul of Beethoven, and another his mind.

Question: *So there may be many incarnations of Beethoven?*

Answer: Yes.

Question: *Is the matter of the different spheres, which have been used to make the body of a great personality, still in the universe? Would it be used in the body of another person who was impressed by that personality?*

Answer: Yes, it will.

Question: *Do the souls on their way to manifestation know that they are to experience life on the physical plane, if that happens to be their destiny, and do they look forward to that experience?*

Answer: They do not distinctly know. They know and they do not know. There is an impulse to go forward, and to experience what they may be able to experience, and to know what they will be able to know, and to reach the place which they may be able to reach. It is that power which [blank] those who are able to advance enough to reach the physical sphere; they manifest as human beings.

Question: *Please explain how to understand why the elephant has such a thick skin in tropical country.*

Answer: In order to protect it from the hot sun, and against the wear and tear in the forests.

Question: *If the* jinn *plane is so beautiful and pure, how is it that any jinn coming to earth could be deeply impressed with evil, so that he became on earth what we might term a devil? Where does the* jinn *learn the evil?*

Answer: The path of the *jinn* is the path of beauty. But it is not only the path of *jinn*; the path of every soul is the path of beauty. Every good soul and bad soul is seeking after beauty. When it steps wrongly in the pursuit of beauty, we call it wrong, and the contrary. As said in the Qur'an: "God is beautiful, and he loves beauty."[14]

13

THE SOULS who are impressed in the *jinn* world by the personalities of those they meet on their way toward manifestation have differences in the nature of the impressions they receive. Some are deeply impressed by one personality and some are slightly impressed; some souls have many impressions in that plane and it is hardly distinguishable which impression is more and which less. However, one thing is true, that one impression is predominant in every soul.

The soul, so to speak, conceives this impression, an impression which is not only the outline of the personality which has impressed it, but the very essence of that personality which this soul has absorbed. Besides, a soul may not be compared with an object, for the soul is all the life there is. Therefore, it does not only take an impression like a photographic plate, it becomes nurtured with it. The soul is creative; therefore, it expresses all that it has absorbed on its way.

The question whether *jinns* are sent on some mission to human beings on earth may be answered: "Yes, whether angel or *jinn* or man, all are intended to play a part in the scheme of the working of the whole universe, and all are used by the wisdom of God for that purpose for which they are created." No doubt the angels are for the angelic plane, *jinns* for the plane of *jinn*, yet the inhabitants of the second and third floor also are sometimes sent to the ground floor on an errand whenever it is necessary.

The most remarkable thing that one can notice in all these planes of existence is that the beings of all these distinct planes are not imprisoned there by the creator. They become captive themselves, just like a man who lives in a village and passes his whole life in that same village. And the story of the neighboring country for him is like telling him about a new world. He never tries to leave his village, and the neighboring country is too foreign to him. He has all his life heard the name of the country but has never made it possible for himself to visit it. It is this nature of the soul, which comes out of its ignorance, that limits it; the soul in point of fact is limitless.

How does a *jinn* soul communicate with human beings on earth? It focuses itself on the heart of man, and experiences all that the man experiences, and knows all that the man knows. It is easy for a *jinn* to do it because its mind is clear like crystal, and it can accommodate and reflect all that falls within its range of vision.

One might ask if the souls on their return journey from earth give their experience to the souls coming from above. But what do the souls coming from above give to the souls on their return journey? They can do a great deal, too, for they know the forgotten ways which they have recently travelled through, and the law, and custom of the way that the souls on the return journey need learn. Besides this, they give them that light and life which is necessary to those worn out and withered souls who have probably given most of themselves to the ever-robbing and consuming plane of the earth. In this way man is helped onward toward his goal by the souls whom he meets on his way in his return journey.

The question in what manner the *jinn* can help man on the earth may be answered that they are capable of inspiring man, not with a definite knowledge of things, but with the sense of the knowledge, especially the knowledge of art and beauty, of tone and rhythm, the knowledge of an inventive nature, and sometimes that knowledge which might help in accomplishing great things in life.

* * *

Question: *How can the soul, which is the divine ray, get worn out and withered?*

Answer: It is not the soul which gets worn out and withered, but it is what it has gathered around it on the earth, what it has imagined itself to be—all that it has taken from the lower planes—that is withered and worn out, not its real self, but its false self.

Question: *Can a soul coming toward the earth ask for help and advice from any soul that particularly interests it, or is it passive?*

Answer: No, he cannot ask for advice or help. His mind is not yet made like a human being's, but he is passive, that is why he gets it without asking. For a child in infancy does not ask for anything, it only wants to have it.

Question: *Does a soul on earth who has a great desire to accomplish something attract a* jinn *to help it? And can the* jinn *make use of him to accomplish something?*

Answer: Yes, both things are possible. A soul may attract a *jinn* to be helped on earth and a *jinn* may attract a soul to accomplish something that it wants to accomplish.

Question: *Why is the* jinn *sufficiently interested in the thing he is going to accomplish on the earth?*

Answer: There is no interest for a *jinn* to accomplish anything on earth. But when it sees what is going on on earth, it becomes interested. A person who does not go out of the house has no interest in the outside, but if a window opens, he has interest.

Question: *What visible difference is there between a* jinn *sent on earth and a* jinn-*like human being?*

Answer: There is no resemblance there; a *jinn* who is in the *jinn* plane is quite distinct as a *jinn*. The real jinn is in the *jinn* plane, and the *jinn* being, a human being, is no more a *jinn* but a human being. But one thing is true, that a soul who is most impressed by the *jinn* plane, that soul has much of the *jinn* plane. When that soul has come on earth, even in the face and features that soul will show something of the *jinn*, even on earth.

Even a soul coming from the angelic plane, and most impressed by the angelic plane, that soul will have in his form and nature and character something about the *jinn* if it be *jinn*, or something of the angel if it be angel. There is something in common in the human face and features, and when there is something uncommon, just some little thing, that is a sign of another world. Also in the nature and character: if that nature and character are in common, it is just like every human being. If there is something uncommon, then that is the sign of the *jinn* plane or of the angelic plane; in short, the face, features, voice, word, character, or nature that show something uncommon, something out of the ordinary.

Question: *Can we say "higher" or "lower" of planes?*

Answer: "Higher" we may say for our convenience, but "higher" as preferable we cannot say. We do not know what is preferable. I should say that the human plane is preferable to all, because there is the sum total of all, the fulfillment of all. Therefore, the person who shows a ripened human personality, that is a thing which is desirable. But at the same time, everything uncommon has some attraction. There is something very beautiful in it, something to admire and observe.

Question: *Does not the idea that worlds of the angel and* jinn *are enriched by experience rising up from life on earth suggest that the being of God also may be affected and recreated this way?*

Answer: The being of God is a perfect being. The riches that the souls bring from the earth by knowledge or by anything are no addition to God; for God it is only that something which is in the hand has come to the elbow. What difference does it make? It is the same. On the other [blank], it is better that the things of the hand be in the hand, not in the elbow. As it is said in the Qur'an: "All the treasure of the earth and the heaven belongs to God." It already exists, it is already in him, the Perfect Being.

Question: *What is the reason of all manifestation? Why does God move the soul from one plane to another?*

Answer: It is his nature. This brings him his satisfaction from the fulfillment of the purpose of the whole creation. But satisfaction is not knowledge, it is something which belongs to him but is brought to fulfillment. In other words, joy is something which belongs to us, but it manifests to us as a result of a certain action. It is not brought by that action, it is in us, it belongs to us, but the action brings us the realization. So the whole creation is an action.

Question: *When God is not creative, does that mean that he is unconscious? Why does God want to be conscious?*

Answer: This creation does not bring something new to God, only it makes him conscious of what he is. Consciousness must have something to become conscious of. Otherwise it is conscience [consciousness?] in essence. A man who is in a dark room with his eyes open—that does not mean that he does not see because his eyes are incapable of seeing, but it means that there is nothing to be seen then. Though the eyes have the capability of seeing, there is nothing to become conscious of seeing. So creation makes God conscious of what he is, conscious of himself.

It is most interesting to watch how that nature of God works in man. For instance sometimes a person begins to walk in a room or to play a drum, or look up and down, and there is no need for it. Why does he do it? Because the absence of action has the effect of paralyzing the activity of the mind, and when the absence of activity has paralyzed the mind, then the soul begins to feel lonely; it begins to wonder whether it is living or not living. And when it begins to tap or to walk, then it realizes, "No, no, I am living!" because it lives in the outward consciousness of life. If we think about this more, it opens up a vast field of knowledge;

this thought will give the deepest knowledge possible. God's desire is to feel himself.

Question: *Is it restlessness?*

Answer: Restlessness in the case of man, but if it is God, it is activity.

Question: *Is it true that the more civilized a man is, the more restless he is?*

Answer: There are two things: there is weakness and there is strength. Both make a person active. Weakness can make a person always keep some activity, but also strength and inspiration make one do something, accomplish something. When a person is weak, his body once put in motion acts and acts without any control. But there is another side, that is strength. These two things are quite different.

Question: *When God is not conscious, is he nothing?*

Answer: Why nothing? How can anything come out of nothing? When we are not doing some active work, we are doing a still greater work. In sleep we are sometimes conscious in our own being. When God is unconscious, he is conscious in his own being.

Question: *Could the consciousness of the soul raise the atoms of the body to such a degree that the body could be maintained beyond man's present belief?*

Answer: Yes.

14

[Editor's Note: *The following questions and answers come from a Question and Answer class given on the same date as the previous lecture. As in the other questions and answers, there is not a single theme, but since many of these questions and answers have some relation to the subject of the soul, the entire class is included here.*]

Question: *As music plays an important part in the higher spheres, should it not be good to have music in the education and to teach it every day, before the beginning of every other thing?*

Answer: I believe so. I think music can be the foundation in training of children, and on that foundation whatever is built will stand firm. Life is rhythm and life is tone. What is music? Music is rhythm and tone, and if a child learns music, he learns the divine language. And if a child has intuition later in life, whatever work he does, he will express in some way that which has been the foundation of his character; in other words, his life will become music.

Question: *Why must certain things about the message and the Sufi Movement not be talked about? Why this secretness?*

Answer: When Wagner was told his music did not appeal to people, it would have been better if he had waited till the king of Bavaria had selected appreciative people. For everything there is a time. There will come a day when the world will appreciate the message the Sufi Movement has to give. Then, no secrecy. We do not tell our little children everything. Every stage prepares the growing child to appreciate, understand and use certain things rightly. So with the secrecy of the Sufi Movement, we must practice ourselves and give others the benefit. Then they will say, where have you got it, what is it? Then tell them, for when they are not ready, there is no use telling. They would only laugh and you would be discouraged and downhearted. There are many in the Order who have just come, and they talked with friends not ready to understand, who were frightened and could not stand it. When these friends were against it, they could not stand firm. So in every thing of value there is a certain amount of secrecy. You do not put your jewels in the street, you keep them safely; it is something you value. So all that is precious is kept treasured and valued. Besides, secrecy has a great blessing.

Suppose a person had the idea that he would invent something wonderful. And he saw the possibility of an invention, and he talked to his family; they could not understand, they laughed at it, and they thought this man is mad. Then he talked to friends and they thought the same. He was discouraged again, and the same with acquaintances also. He had an idea in advance of his age, but in the end he was so impressed by the idea of madness that he could not realize it, whether mad or not.

There are many pessimistic people, many discouraging people, who have envy and jealousy, many who cannot understand, who are too proud, too vain to stand anyone doing anything better. Human nature has its weak side. So wise people do not talk about what they value. They give the seed a chance to take root and come up, and when it bears its fruit, then let people see it. Secrecy works like a fence round little plants. When they are small, chickens will eat them, dogs and cats root them up, but the fence will protect them till the stem is strong. Now our movement is delicate; like an infant it must be protected from every thing, even from the evil eye that may fall upon the little infant if it is not protected.

In the past, with the great masters—how their works have been spoilt. Even before the coming of Jesus Christ, the prophesies spoilt his mission. Herod[15] was frightened, and before the Master could work, he was put out of the country; no chance was given to him.

When something valuable is done, there is always criticism and jealousy. The best way of protection is the noiseless worker. What do we care if anyone recognizes us? We only care if we are able to do our sacred duty, our sacred work, unknown. We should be most thankful if no one knew us and we accomplished our work. Have there not come great people artists, musicians, etc.? Are there not many more than those whose names we know? What a great beauty there is in being unknown. There is remembrance of the unknown soldier; everyone goes with flowers for the unknown soldier. That ideal we should cherish in our hearts, that is what we are concerned with, and the less noise we make the more we shall accomplish.

Question: *You told us the other day there is not such a thing as sadness.*[16] *But why did Christ say "My soul is full of sadness" and also "my Father, why hast Thou abandoned me!" Is this not a tragedy? And is there not a tragedy in life?*

Answer: We must know, above and beyond all, the Master's human side of life, his divine side apart. And if the human side were not human, then why has God sent a message to human beings by a man? Why should he not send it by angels? Because a human being knows human beings, because he knows human limitation. That is the most beautiful side of the Master's life. If he did not feel sadness, how could he sympathize with others? If all were perfect, why be born on earth? The purpose is that from limitation we grow towards perfection. If from childhood all were wise, why did we come? Beauty is in acquiring wisdom by failure, mistake. All suffering in life, all is worth while and all accomplishes the purpose of our coming on earth.

Question: *Do other planets get their messengers too?*

Answer: Yes, they do.

Question: *If music is rhythm, why are so many musicians so unbalanced in temper and in temperament?*

Answer: Is it not beautiful to have a little temper? Temper is a rhythm. A person who does not fight at least once a week does not live; it is human to have faults; the joy is in overcoming. Music is not all sadness or all joy; music is earth and heaven. Music is greater than heaven because it takes in earth and heaven too.

Question: *An occultist said, "No occultist can be without a sense of humor." Do you agree with this, and what is the meaning of humor?*

Answer: I quite agree. Humor is the sign of light, light from above. When that light touches the mind, it tickles it, and it is the tickling of the mind that produces humor.

Question: *What do you mean by the evil eye?*

Answer: The evil eye is the eye of bitterness, jealousy, opposition; the eye that looks at objects with the thought: may this object be destroyed, or: why does it exist? It is an eye behind which is a mind, and that mind is poisonous. And you must know that for everything that is good, valuable, and precious, there is always some evil eye to look at it.

Question: *Does it make any difference where the soul going towards manifestation meets with the returning soul? Is it in the angelic plane impressed by feelings, and in the* jinn *plane more particularly by mind and intelligence?*

Answer: Yes, it is impressed by both; in the *jinn* world and angelic world, both.

Question: *Some people cannot eat meat because they think that to kill is against the law of life. Is this feeling of theirs true or an illusion?*

Answer: It is true. It is an illusion as far as truth can be an illusion, but beyond the limit of illusion it is true.

Question: *How long does the departed soul remain with his beloved one? Will a mother be able to guide her young children till they are grown up?*

Answer: Yes, if she wants to.

Question: *Why are women more attracted by devotion than men?*

Answer: The mother nature of woman is more responsible for human beings than man, naturally. If it were not for the love of the mother, the world could not go on, and it is that principle which is devotion. So the quality of devotion in woman is the secret of the whole creation.[17]

Question: *Are women better than men?*

Answer: It is very difficult to make a line. Once a person asked me: I have heard the [blank][18] believed that women possess no soul. I said, yes they have every reason for this belief, for they know that woman is soul itself.

Question: *Does a soul who has once touched the earth go up and down from the earth through the* jinn *plane to the angelic plane, and from the angelic plane through the* jinn *plane to the earth?*

Answer: Yes, only it depends what evolution the soul has reached.

Question: *Children who die young, do they go to heaven or do they return to earth?*

Answer: I have not yet spoken on the subject of the soul's return, and it is such a vast subject that I shall not touch it.

Question: *The souls who manifest on earth, must they attain perfection on the earth, or can they also attain it on the journey towards the goal?*

Answer: Yes, it can be attained on the journey to the goal also, but I should think that what is done today is better than tomorrow; if we can realize perfection today, it is better than waiting to attain it in the hereafter.

Question: *You spoke of* prana *as the central breath. Will you explain what that means?*

Answer: There is a river and there are many streams branching out from the river; they are small rivers, too. And so is breath one central breath and many other breaths. One breath keeps the mechanism of the whole body going, but there are many other breaths, which, for instance, help in contraction, expansion. Sneezing or yawning or blinking the eyes, all these come from a certain direction of a little breath, a stream branching from the central breath, which works as a battery behind all the mechanism, actions and movements in the body.

Question: *Can a soul choose its place of birth and its family?*

Answer: Yes, it does choose nearly always.

THE SOUL'S JOURNEY

TOWARDS MANIFESTATION

THE MANIFESTED SOUL

TOWARDS THE GOAL

THE MANIFESTED SOUL

15

As THE SOUL passes through the plane of the *jinn*, it arrives in the physical spheres. What helps this soul to come to the physical plane? What opens the way for this new-coming soul to enter physical existence? The souls on earth. The coming soul enters the physical spheres by the channel of the breath. Breath, which is the power at the back of every action, works as a battery which keeps the physical mechanism of the human body going. The secret of birth and death is to be found in the mystery of breath. What is Cupid? It is the soul which is being born, before it appears on the physical plane. It is pictured by the wise as a cupid, an angel. It is an angel, for the soul is the angel.

Duality in every aspect of life and in whatever plane is creative, and its issue is the purpose, the outcome of the dual aspect of nature. The affinity which brings about the fulfilment of the purpose is the phenomenon of Cupid; in reality it is the phenomenon of the soul. When the soul is born on earth, its first expression is a cry. Why does it cry? Because it finds itself in a new place which is all strange to it. It finds itself in a captivity which it did not experience before. Every person, every object is something new, something foreign to this soul, but soon this condition passes away.

No sooner do the senses of the infant become acquainted with the outer life, which so continually attracts its attention, than it first becomes interested in breathing the air of the world; then it becomes interested in hearing the sounds; then it becomes interested in seeing objects before it; then it becomes interested in touching, and then it develops its taste.

The more familiar the soul becomes with this physical world, the more interested it becomes, though sometimes it shows homesickness in the fits of crying that it so often gets during its infancy. It is not always illness; it is not always that it is crying for things outside. No doubt as it grows, it longs for things outside of itself, but it is a feeling of having been removed from a place which was more pleasant and comfortable, and having come to a foreign land of which it knows so little. It is this which brings the infant fits of crying.

The wisdom of nature is perfect, and there is no better vision of divine splendor than an infant in its early infancy. Imagine, if the senses of an infant were as developed as the senses of a grown- up person, it would have lost its mind from the sudden pressure of the physical world falling instantly upon it. Its delicate senses would not be able to withstand the pressure of so many and various and intense activities of this world. How the wisdom behind it, which is the evidence of that divine protector, Father and Mother, the creator who is the support and protection of all, works so that gradually the senses of the child develop. The more familiar the infant becomes with life the more its senses are developed, and the more it knows the more its mind develops. And it cannot know more than its mind can grasp, so that in every way the infant is protected, its body and mind both.

* * *

Question: *Can you tell us something about twins? Why are they not always united on earth?*

Answer: They were meant to be united. If twins are twins in the real sense of the word, i.e. if two twin souls have started the whole journey and have managed to come together to earth, they are most united. I have known two twins so united that if one had an illness, the other had an illness; if

one was happy, the other was happy even if they were separated. But then there could be two persons walking in the
rain and finding some shelter, who happened to arrive in the
same place; that is another thing.

But there may be two souls, born in different countries,
brought up by different parents, and yet they would attract
one another, would supply to one another what is needed
in their lives. They can be best friends, they can be good
partners, or be in the capacity of master and servant.

Question: *What is the difference between magnetism and
electric current?*

Answer: There is not much difference because scientists
have never been able to give an answer to what electricity
is. Is electricity magnetism? Is magnetism electricity? If any-
body were to ask me, I would say they are the same thing.
The power of attracting: magnetism; the power that gives
force and energy: electricity. But it is the same power.

Question: *Is the affinity which brings two human beings
together in love always the soul working behind it?*

Answer: Certainly.

Question: *Why are some souls born in miserable surroundings?*

Answer: There is a saying in the Qur'an which has been mis-
interpreted: "The creation has come out of darkness." The
soul is not always coming with open eyes. It is coming with
closed eyes, the picture of which the infant shows, whose
eyes open afterwards. But at the same time to compare our
condition with other conditions one needs to be familiar
with conditions, and that time comes after being born. If this
question will be considered more deeply, one will come to
a very great realization of the secret of life, and especially of
good fortune and bad fortune; that it is not always a design
in which the soul is so limited that it cannot get out of it, but
that every soul makes for itself a condition, even after coming on earth.

Are there not thousands who live in miserable, in bad

conditions, because they have known no better? If they had known better, they would have managed to become better. This rule applies to many persons in life. Most of the reasons for misery are in their own ignorance. If they knew how to combat, how to get out of misery, there are many doors, many ways to get out of it. To me, just now, it does not seem unfair whatever the bad condition of a person, because I see that his gains have equal losses and his losses have equal gains. It sums up. Only we do not see how it costs and whether it costs first or last or in the middle. And outward conditions count little.

Question: *Are men and women always separate or are they two halves of an entity which has been separated and has to be reestablished?*

Answer: You may call them two parts of one soul, but really speaking we are all parts of one soul and all long to unite in one soul. At the same time there are affinities, affinities of the *jinn* plane, of the angelic plane, of the human plane, many different ties, many different affinities of soul which attract them to one another.

Question: *Why does a spiritist go into a trance?*

Answer: He must die in order to reach the dead. That is the condition.

Question: *The center of a child's head closes at seven years. Is it true to say that he loses sight of the other spheres then?*

Answer: This is definitely said. I would only say that as the child grows and loses that innocence of childhood, so it seems to be removed from the angelic world.

Question: *How do you explain that the physical body shows signs of evolution through the animal kingdom?*

Answer: In short, in this series I am trying to explain the human soul and its connection with the physical world. This subject will come afterwards also.

16

WHEN THE SOUL comes in the physical world, it receives an offering, an offering from the whole universe, an offering from the whole world, and that offering is the body in which to function. It is not offered to the soul by the parents but by the ancestors, by that nation, by that race into which the soul is born and by the whole human race.

This body is not only an offering of the human race but it is an outcome of something that the world has produced for ages, a clay which has been kneaded a thousand times over, a clay which was prepared so that in its every development it has become more intelligent, more radiant and more living, a clay which appeared first in the mineral kingdom, which developed then in the vegetable kingdom, which then appeared in the animal kingdom and which was finished in the making of that body which is offered to the newcoming soul.

One may ask whether it is not true then, as some scientists say in their biological study, that man has risen from the animal kingdom. Certainly it is true, but true in the sense as explained above. In order to come to the world of human beings, a soul need not be an animal and then develop itself in man. We need not understand by this that every rock turned into a plant and every plant became an animal and every animal turned into man. The soul is direct from heaven; it itself functions in a body, and it is this body through which it experiences life on the earth more fully. Rocks and trees and animals, therefore, may not be considered as the ancestors of the soul. It is the body which is the outcome of the working of all these different kingdoms, which are the development of one another.

A question arises, "Why must a soul function in a human body? Why not in an animal, in a bird, in an insect?" The answer is that it does. Every soul is not the same ray, has not the same degree of illumination, has not the same far-reaching power. And therefore, it is true that souls do not always function in a human body, but souls have functioned in all forms which seem living, however insignificant and small. The question then arises, "What about rocks and mountains, and what about the sea and the river? Where have they come from? Are they not all the outcome of the soul?" And the answer is that nature in general, in its different aspects, is the materialization of that light which is called spirit, the Divine Spirit.

But has it a soul, has everything in nature a soul? The answer is, not in the sense of the word we understand by soul. For we recognize that ray which has functioned in the human body as a soul. We do not recognize the ray which has functioned in the lower creation to be the same, although it is a ray which has come from the same source. There are two things: there are rays and there is light. If the rays are the souls of beings, then the light of the same divine sun is the spirit of the whole of nature. It is the same light; it is the same spirit, only not divided and not distinct as the rays which we call souls.

But the question is, "Why has nature its different aspects?" There is earth and there is water and there are mountains and there is sea. If the spirit behind it is one, why is it all distinct and different? And the answer is that creation is a gradual evolution of that light which is the source and goal of all things. For instance, plant life is a development of the mineral kingdom of the earth. Animal life is the development of the vegetable kingdom. Human life is the culmination of this evolution. But this culmination is the finishing of that vehicle which the soul uses. By this evolution the soul is not evolved; by this evolution it is only meant that the soul has adopted a more finished instrument to experience life more fully. No doubt, the better the instrument of experience, the greater is the satisfaction of the soul. When one looks from this point of view at the whole creation, one feels like saying that not only man but the whole manifestation was created in the image of God.

* * *

Question: *Why does part of the light become rays or human souls and the other part remain plants and animals?*

Answer: No, I did not mean that the other part remains plants and animals. I have only said that where there is no individual appearance, separate appearance, but where there is a mass of matter before us, as a lake or river or mountain, there we see the light of the same divine sun, and in its radiant form there is intelligence also. But the ray is a kind of straight living current, and it is this living current functioning in a more developed body that is able to produce that experience which is the fulfilment of the whole creation.

As soon as the trees begin to appear as separate trees, no doubt they are separate rays; it is most difficult to differentiate rays from the light and light from the rays; it is more for our convenience. Through the rays it is more distinct, more separate; in the form of light it is more together. And therefore, all that is before our eyes as something connected together, that is the phenomenon of that light; and all that shows out as an entity, that is expressive of the ray.

But at the same time one must remember that the truth cannot be put into words. What one can do is to make, as much as possible, an effort to make the mystery of life more intelligible to the mind; therefore, "light" and "ray" and "sun" are used. But it must be seen in the light of one's own intuition; then this problem will become clear to one's sight.

Question: *Why do some rays become trees, some human beings?*

Answer: Some rays fall having functioned upon the body, and some rays, not having so functioned, become the trees.

Take for instance the example of the rain: Why must the raindrops rear the poisonous plants and weeds? Why should it not fall only upon the corn and the plants and fruits and flowers? The rain falls on all things, on more useful and less useful plants. So do the rays from there. Some fall on the streets, some on the rock, some on the fertile soil, and there they grow. If we picture it as a divine rain, then this divine rain, falling in the form of light, takes in everything that there is, and raises out of it all that comes.

Question: *Can you please explain when and how the difference in the development of the soul comes in the different kingdoms?*

Answer: The body is not dead matter; it is matter with spirit. That spirit is light. One cannot make a very great distinction between the differences and the grades of light. If the degree of the light of a soul were not developed to a certain mark of the body that it would meet on its way to expression, it would not take it and would only be attracted to another body, with another mark.

There are numerous differences between the rays. Rays are first expressed, and then they fall upon all that meets them. The differences of the rays are they are not of the same grade of intenseness, of illumination, of expression. Souls are first expressed; there is nothing to attract them. Then influences come and the souls go where they are attracted, to the mineral, the vegetable, the animal or the human kingdom. The ray that falls in the human kingdom is more intense and direct.

Question: *How can you see the kingdom of God in all manifestation?*

Answer: If you develop your eyes to see, you can see. For instance, what man thinks, he sees. All man sees is his own thought. Man can produce out of his thought a ghost, or a satan, or a devil. And out of his thought he can produce God, the most merciful and compassionate. When man has come to the realization of that one who is the source and the goal, and that all is developing to that goal, then he begins to see that that goal is God; and in all things he begins to see that goal. Therefore, he calls it God. Then it all becomes one, it is unity, it is God. There is no more variety.

Question: *Is the attraction from the body towards the ray or soul entirely by accident? Is there not an element of justice?*

Answer: The idea of justice is based upon good and bad. Where there is justice, there is injustice; that means there are two. Truth is only one. The idea of justice and injustice is from man's conception. When a person rises above justice and injustice—which is subject to change in his every evolution—when he gets above this, he will reach the knowledge of truth.

Fairness and unfairness belong to our particular evolution. The less intelligent, the more fairness and unfairness man sees and thinks about. A stupid person is always ready to judge. In heaven there is only one truth, and truth is one. And where there is no comparison, there is no fairness and no unfairness. Something is greater than fairness and unfairness and that is the truth. It cannot be explained. Truth cannot be acquired, only discovered. Man is not born with judging.

Question: *Is the doctrine of reincarnation not a missing link in the understanding of the attraction of the rays by the different kingdoms?*

Answer: Sufism is not against any doctrine. A message which has come to reconcile, must it oppose any doctrine? In India you will hardly find a man speaking about reincarnation. He will only speak about the result of the *karma*. All we have learned about reincarnation comes from theosophical sides. If you ask a Yogi about it, he says, "No, I am starving for mukti, for freedom; it is you who will be born again." To whom does he point—you? The Buddhist also says that Buddha has never spoken about reincarnation. It is not that it is a wrong doctrine, for I don't see the wrong of it, but where is the right of it? The purpose of life is realizing God and losing from one's mind the false self. If that is the purpose, then the theory of reincarnation is based upon the conception of the false ego.

It is true that punishment comes from your bad actions. But what are you? And which action will bring which result? Who can tell it? What is apparent is different from what is hidden.

I do not mean that the doctrine of reincarnation is wrong, but what is the right of it? It is based upon the false ego. Where is the right of something which is based upon the false ego, and against which all religions have taught? Jesus Christ taught the everlasting life. Muhammad taught *hadyat* equals liberation, and in Hinduism the *mukti* seeks freedom from the falsehood of the soul.[19] It is against my object, which is to wave it off from your vision and to keep before your vision the idea of unity, in which we all unite and in which lies the fulfilment of life.

17

THE SOUL who has already brought with it from the angelic plane a luminous body upon the plane of *jinns*, a body full of impressions, functions in the end in the human body which the physical plane offers it, and settles for some time in this abode. This completes what we understand by the word individuality. These three planes, which are the principal planes of existence, are called in the terms of Vedanta *triloka*, which means three worlds: *bhu lok*, meaning the physical world; *gandharva lok*, meaning the world of *jinns*; and *deva lok*, the world of angels. The human being, therefore, has all three beings in him, the angel, the *jinn* and man.

What man acquires on the earth is the experience which he makes by the means of his senses, an experience which he himself makes. And it is this experience which man collects in that accommodation within himself which he calls the heart. And after this is collected, that surface of the heart, which is the collection of his knowledge, he calls the mind. This word comes from *mana* in Sanskrit, which means mind, and from this word the word man has come.

The question is, "How far does he recollect the memory of the angelic world and of the *jinn* world?" He shows the memory of the angelic world and of the *jinn* world by his tendencies: his tendency for light, for the truth, for love, for righteousness. His love of God, his seeking for the truth of life, this all shows the angel in him. In appreciating beauty, in drawing towards art, in love for music, appreciation for poetry, the tendency to produce, to create, to express—all this shows in him the sign of the *jinn* world.

The impressions which constitute his being, which he has brought as a heritage from the *jinn* world, which have been imparted to him from the souls on their way back towards the goal, he shows also as something different and peculiar to what his people possess. No doubt it often happens that a child possesses qualities of his ancestors, which were, perhaps, missing in his parents or even two, three generations back. However, this is another heritage, a heritage which is known to us as such.

I might just as well say that the soul borrows a property, a property from the *jinn* world and a more concrete property from the physical world. And as it borrows this property, together with this transaction, it takes upon itself the taxation and the obligations besides the responsibility which is attached to this property. Very often the property is not in proper repair and damage has been done to it, and it falls to his lot to repair it; and if there be a mortgage on that property, that becomes his lot. Together with the property, he becomes the owner of the records and the contracts and the papers of that property which he owns. In this is to be found the secret of what is called, in the language of the Hindus, *karma*.

What makes the soul know of its own existence? Something with which it adorns itself, something which it adopts, possesses, owns and uses. For instance, what makes the king know that he is a king? His palace, his kingly environment, people standing before him in attendance. If that were all absent, the soul would be no king. Therefore, the king is a palace. It is the consciousness of the environment which makes the soul feel, "I am so and so." What it adorns itself with, that makes it say, "I am this or that." If not, by origin it is something nameless, formless. On the earth plane the personality develops out of individuality. The soul is an individual from the moment it has been born on the earth, in the worldly sense of the word. But it becomes a person as it grows, for personality is the development of individuality, and in personality, which is built by building character, is born that spirit which is the rebirth of the soul. The first birth is the birth of man, the next birth is the birth of God.

* * *

Question: *Is there a likeness between the angel body, the jinn body and the physical body of a person?*

Answer: No definite design of that likeness may be made, but they are all developing towards the image of man, which is called in the scriptures, "after the image of God." Only what may be said is this: that the physical body is most distinct and clear; the *jinn* body is less distinct, more phantom-like; and the angelic body is still less distinct, but less distinct to the physical eyes. And therefore, one cannot make a similarity between the things of the earth and the things of the other world. If there is any similarity, it is that the whole manifestation is a development towards the human image, and that truth can be found even in the study of natural science and biology.

Question: *There is something peculiarly vivid about one's earlier recollections of childhood. Is there any special reason for this?*

Answer: We repeat after coming on earth the same process through which the soul has passed: infancy is expressive of the angelic world; then childhood is expressive of the *jinn* world; youth is expressive of the human world; and when one passes on, one gets closer again to the higher spheres.

Question: *Are the differences of the rays going to the different kingdoms not differences in the grade of individualization?*

Answer: When they start from there, they are not marked with individualization. But as they go further they are influenced in each step to take that particular direction. For instance, a child was born; then he went to see a play. He liked it so much that he became an artist. That was the second thing. That means one step helps another step; in this way the soul's direction becomes changed.

Question: *Are they not produced by differences of time, that means differences in age?*

Answer: Of course difference of time causes difference of age.

Question: *Are those differences produced by difference of time, the difference of evolution of the soul? A soul who is more individualized, is it a longer time ago that he came from God?*

Answer: No, it has nothing to do with time. It is according to the strength and light and volume of the ray that the individuality is more complete and more perfect.

Question: *If it has nothing to do with time, does that mean that time does not exist?*

Answer: Yes, time does not exist, but here it means that the attraction from the soul towards its body of manifestation has nothing to do with time.

In the angelic world there is a distinction of three kinds: of volume of radiance, of light, and of shortness and length of life. In the *jinn* world comes the attraction to form. From there evolution is a different thing. The attraction to forms is from the *jinn* world. For instance, if a man is a thief, that is because he became a thief in the *jinn* world; there he was impressed by theft.

Question: *But what makes a soul impressed by one thing and not by another?*

Answer: Its grade of evolution, its volume, and its light.

Question: *Is meditation to be compared with a hothouse?*

Answer: If our life were not so artificial, we would not need meditation or religion. Every soul is born with the capacity to draw all the bliss that is necessary for it. Therefore, in the time of the ancient people, they had their way of drawing that ecstasy.

The more artificial we become, the more there comes a need of religion and meditation that we may connect ourselves with that object which is needed for our evolution. If it were not so, it would be very unfair and unjust to the birds and animals that man should have that exaltation and the birds and animals who have done nothing wrong should be deprived of it. But that is not so. We are deprived of it because we have deprived ourselves of it. Nature gives all the bliss that is necessary for our soul. But having developed in ourselves such an unnatural way of nature and habits of living, we cannot draw that bliss which the animals and birds can draw.

Question: *Does the individuality end or does it improve?*

Answer: It improves.

Question: *Then God's gain after creation is a gain in individuality, in power to create (for individuality equals vanity equals power to express)?*

Answer: To some extent, but God is perfect; you cannot say there is a gain for God.

Question: *Does a soul travel from plane to plane and vice versa?*

Answer: Yes, this is true, but from the spiritual point of view it is not true, for the soul does not travel; the soul is always in God, the soul itself is God. Instead of saying that the soul travels, we can rightly say that God travels. Traveling means losing consciousness in one plane and awakening in another plane, but is not moving for the soul. The soul does not travel; the soul remains in God, though the principle of individualization is in God.

Though the individuality begins in the Divine Spirit, the oneness is so great that we cannot say it is the same soul, though it is the same "I-ness." It is also not the soul who reincarnates, it is the soul that gains and loses consciousness on the different planes; it is its vehicle of consciousness on the different planes which reincarnates.

The thing is that the whole puzzle is solved by solving the question who is "I"? "I" is God himself. With time, it is the same as with the bodily form. It does not exist. All here is a play of shadows. In the sentence, "I slept in the mineral, I stirred in the vegetable, I dreamed in the animal, I awoke in man," who is "I"? It is God who says this.

Now, there is a question of time from the human point of view. Yes, from the human point of view there is time, but from the spiritual point of view there is not. The question that all souls have a sum total of difficulties which is the same means the sum total of their difficulties in the shadows. The only living moment in this world of shadows is the now. Past and future do not really exist.

But can the past be changed? Yes, it can. The past can be changed. That is the whole key to the understanding of this illusion. Two things have to be understood in this: one, to utilize matter to its best advantage; two, to rise above matter.

Why is the past dead? Because dead is that which does not have a real existence. The shadow is dead, not the light, the light has only disappeared.

Why does God live only in the moment of now and not in the past and in the future? Because God is eternal, and the life of the moment is his fullest experience. The past can be changed by making oneself independent from its horrible effect. The thing is that one must deny what one does not want to have.

The secret is that God's mind only lives, and not the minds of mankind, which are doing acts of shadows. To live means for man his only chance to focus his mind in God's mind.

The whole secret is that things which belong to the earth and things which belong to heaven cannot be compared; i.e. one moment of the *jinn* world is equal to a hundred years of this world, and a hundred years of the *jinn* world is equal to one moment of the angelic world. There is no comparison.

Question: *Is it possible for a soul to reach divine perfection after having been only once on the earth?*

Answer: Yes.

Question: *Does this sometimes happen?*

Answer: Very often.

Question: *But is it not the way of the multitude?*

Answer: No, it is not everyone's way.

Question: *Can one change one's way and go quicker?*

Answer: One can change, it only depends on oneself.

18

THE LAW that governs the soul's manifestation may be divided into three parts: that of the angelic world; of the world of *jinn;* and of the world of man, or of the physical world.

In the angelic world there are no distinct impressions but there is a tuning. The soul is tuned to a certain pitch by the law of vibrations, high or low, according to the impressions it receives from the souls coming back home. In this tuning it gets, so to speak, a tone and a rhythm which directs its path towards the world of the *jinn.*

Souls in themselves are not different in the angelic world, as it is immediately next to the Divine Being. If there is a difference in the souls there in the angelic world, it is the difference of more or less radiance and a longer or a shorter scope of their run. The law that attracts the souls from the *jinn* world to the human world is all that they receive from the souls who are bound homeward. In accordance with this, they take their direction towards the physical world.

If I were to give this idea in a more expressive form, I would say it is like a person whose heart is tuned to love and light and to appreciate and to admire. He will certainly take a direction towards a greater beauty and will seek such friends to meet with and learn from, who would seem to him in some way similar to his nature or ideal. This is an example of the soul which is attracted from the angelic world to the *jinn* world. A person who has studied music and practices through his life will certainly seek the association of musical friends, the artists, the singers, the composers, the lovers of music. Among them he will find his friends, his comrades. So a soul from the *jinn* world is directed according to its love for certain things in the physical world. This shows that God does not thrust certain conditions upon souls going towards manifestation, but in this manner they choose them.

A person may ask, "No soul must have chosen for itself a miserable condition. How then do some souls happen to be born in miserable conditions?"[20] The answer to this we find before us in this world. Many in this world often cause their own miseries. They may not know it; they may not admit it. Nevertheless, many of our joys and sorrows are caused by ourselves.

By this I do not mean to say that this is the only law that governs life. No, this is a law in answer to the question that rises out of common sense. But if one raised one's head from this world of illusion and looked up and asked, "Tell me the secret and the mystery of your creation," one will hear in answer that every thing and being is placed in its place, and each is busy carrying out that work which is to be done in the whole scheme of nature. Life is a symphony, and the action of every person in this symphony is the playing of his part, his particular part in this music.

If there is anything which will give peace, it is the understanding of this. The thought, "I am suffering now because of my sins in the past life," may bring an answer to the inquiring and reasoning mind to stop it from dispute for the moment. But will this take away that irritation that the misery is causing in his heart? Will that mind ever excuse God for having so severely judged him? Yes, he will own his mistakes of the past, but he will never believe in God as a God of love and compassion, as a God of kindness and mercy, and as a God of forgiveness.

* * *

Question: *You said once that the sum total of every person's difficulties is the same. For what period of life did you mean this, for one earthly life, or for the time during the journey towards manifestation, and from one manifestation or from a still greater period of existence?*

Answer: The sum total is what we can call the horizon. But if we had to point out which is the horizon and where it is, we cannot. But as we go to the horizon, we find the diminishing of the cause and effect and sum it up in one life. The further we reach, the closer we come to that equilibrium which is shown by that sign of the tail of the serpent in its mouth. Neither is there tail nor mouth. For when the serpent has curled itself and put its tail in its mouth, then it is perfect.

For instance, there was a man who once hated his neighbor. He quarreled and fought with him and took revenge. There were fights and quarrels, and they exchanged their ill will towards one another, used words against one another. In the end the heart of one person was melted, and he said, "What are we quarreling about? It is nothing, just a misunderstanding. I am so sorry." The whole thing, which was built into a mountain, dropped in a moment. Nothing of the past was left. They became friends and loved one another.

There comes a moment, and that moment is every moment, and as we go on so there come moments when things sum up. There is the finishing of it. As we go further, so more finishes. All our disputes and arguments about the differences and distinctions, about high and low, good and bad, all fade away as we go further. They become so faded away that no color is left. Then there will come white light which is the light of God. It is that attainment which Buddha has called *nirvana*. *Vana* means color; *nir*, no; it means "no color." What is color? That is green, this is blue, this is high, this is low, this is right, this is wrong. All colors, for our common sense, become a property, a reality, but in the realm of truth they fade away, they have no existence.

It is not an intellectual realization; it is living it. If someone runs away with your hat, you run after him and he says, "It is mine, it is not yours." That is the test, whether he has the *nirvana*. But there are the blessed souls, the souls who are really satisfied, whose hunger is really satisfied when they see another person having eaten his dinner; their hunger is satisfied. There are such souls living on earth, who by seeing another person adorned in beautiful clothes, are satisfied. Their gladness is to see another person dressed beautifully. It might seem—what a renunciation, self-denial! It is not. They have risen above it. They have gone through a cross. They have arrived at *nirvana*. In such a stage it is no pain; it only gives them pleasure. But the spark of this *nirvana* is in every soul. *Nirvana* is the perfection of that, but the spark is in every soul.

The other day I said to a child, "Would you rather give your toy to the other poor child?" Now that child had just got his toy and had not yet played with it. I saw the face of the child. I said, "Would you be really glad to see another child playing with your toy? You should not give the toy if you would not be glad." And I tell you, it was just like striking a match to a candle, that spark of *nirvana*. The child most willingly went and gave his toy to the poor child. His face was beaming with joy at the happiness of giving it. He was so happy to think that the other child was happy. There was no end to his happiness.

Therefore, it is not something which we must learn; it is in us, but it becomes buried in us. If it were only dug up by our love for it. We need not look for acquiring it. It is not something which we acquire. We must develop it, then it becomes brilliant. Then it consumes all the impurities of life. Call it sin or wrong or a mistake of the past; it is all consumed in that brilliant light. It eats it all up, and turns it into that brilliant light which is divine light.

19

THE SOUL comes on earth rich or poor, ripened or unripened, through three phases where either it is enriched or it has lost its opportunity. It takes light from the angelic world, knowledge from the *jinn* world, and inherits qualities from parents and ancestors.

Of these things that it has collected on its way to its manifestation on the earth is made that accommodation which is called the mind. The body, in which the soul functions in the physical plane, also contributes to the soul properties of all the worlds that it has belonged to: the mineral kingdom, the vegetable kingdom and the animal kingdom. It is therefore that man is called a universe itself; for in man himself consists all that is in heaven and all that is on the earth. "We have made him our *khalif*," says God in the Qur'an, pertaining to man, meaning, "Our representative, our chief, under whose care a universe is given," for man himself is a universe.

Man shows in his life the traces of all the conditions through which the clay has gone, the clay that makes his body. There are atoms of his body which represent the mineral kingdom, the vegetable kingdom, the animal kingdom—all are represented in him. Not only his body, but his mind shows in it the reflection of all the kingdoms through which his body has gone. For the mind is the medium between heaven and earth.

Man experiences heaven when conscious of his soul; he experiences the earth when conscious of the body. Man experiences that plane which is between heaven and the earth when he is conscious of his mind. Man shows by his stupidity the mineral kingdom which is in him, thick and hard. Man shows the vegetable kingdom in him by his pliability, by his inventive and creative faculties which bring forth the flowers and fruits of his life from his actions, thoughts and deeds. Man shows the traces of the animal kingdom in him in his passion, emotion, attachment, in his willingness for service and usefulness. And if one were to say what represents the human in him, the answer is all things, all attributes of the earth and heaven: the stillness, hardness and strength of the stone; the fighting nature and tendency to attachment from the animal; the fruitfulness and usefulness of the vegetable kingdom; the inventive and artistic, poetical and musical genius of the world of *jinns*; the beauty and illumination, love, calm and peace of the angelic planes—all these things put together make man. It is therefore that the human soul consists of all and thus culminates in that purpose for which the whole creation has taken place.

* * *

Question: *Does the soul find the accommodation of the mind when he arrives on earth, or does he make it afterwards?*

Answer: The soul brings on earth an accommodation already made in a very negative state from the world of *jinns;* that is the place where it gets the mold of its mind. The body it gets after coming on the earth. But that accommodation is filled later on, after the soul's wakening on the earth plane. It is here that that accommodation completes itself and becomes the mind.

Question: *Is it only a mold?*

Answer: Yes, a mold with impressions, that is the accommodation. For instance, there is one child who very attentively hears music; there is another child who runs away from it. The child who runs away from it, his mind has not got that mold; music is not engraved there. He will learn it, as he will hear it, but another child, where there is already the mold, is musical. He will be seeking for some music to

114

come in and fit in that mold which is there already.

Question: *You said that the inventive faculty and fruitfulness show the vegetable kingdom in man, but does that not come from his jinn faculty?*

Answer: I beg your pardon, I have not said the inventive faculty comes from fruitfulness; the inventive faculty comes from the *jinn* world.

Question: *Can you explain what makes some souls not able to progress, as if they were dead?*

Answer: I should think the reflection of the mineral kingdom, thickness. That is the only convenient word I can find. For instance, if the sun is thickly clouded, the light does not reach the earth. So with the soul which is divine and has all the light; if that is thickly clouded, then man does not receive the light which is in himself. The light is there, but he does not receive it. What difference is there between a diamond and an ordinary stone? The difference is of thickness. The diamond reflects the light which falls upon it, and the stone is so thick that it will not allow the light to reflect in it. The diamond allows the light of the sun to reflect in it, and the stone does not.

There is a story of a murshid. A mureed went for a long time to the house of the murshid and tried to develop spiritually. But with all his enthusiasm and desire to advance, he remained in the same place. A long time after, he said, "Murshid, I have no more patience now. A long time I have given under your guidance. I do not see any further. I am standing in the same place as before." The murshid felt very embarrassed to hear those words from him, and most sad. He said, "Look here my son, come with me." And the first thing that they met in the street was a mad dog, barking and wanting to bite. Murshid looked at that dog and instantly that dog become sane. He said, "Look here, do you see the change? If the glance of Murshid can do that to an animal who is not accustomed to wisdom, what must it do for a human being like you? But if your doors are closed, what can Murshid's glance do? You are enthusiastic, you are eager, you are willing, but you are not open."

Therefore, it is the openness of heart, it is the response, the responsive attitude that is the principal thing in pupilship. That is what makes one a disciple. That we can learn by seeing the difference between the pebble and the diamond. The pebble does not take the light of the sun, the diamond does. And the question of whether it is the favor or disfavor of the teacher which enlightens the mureed may be answered, that the soul cannot be a murshid who favors and disfavors.

The first condition of being a murshid is to favor, to favor the friend and enemy. There is no lack of favor if a person does not become enlightened; when the rain falls, it falls upon all trees, but according to the response of those trees, they grow and bear fruit. The sun shines upon all trees; it does not make a distinction between this tree or that tree. But in accordance with the absorption of the light which is falling upon them, in accordance to the response that the trees give to the sun, they get it. And remember at the same time, that very often a mureed is an inspiration for the murshid, because it is not the murshid who teaches, it is God who teaches. The murshid is only a medium.

And as high as the response of the mureed reaches, so strongly does it attract the message of God. The mureed can inspire, and the mureed can shut his inspiration too. If there were no response on his side, if there were antagonism on his side, if there were a lack of interest on his side, then the inspiration of Murshid becomes closed. Just like the clouds, when running over the desert, they cannot shower. It is the desert which affects them. And when the clouds come upon the forests, the trees attract and the rain falls.

20

THE SOUL, manifested on the earth, is not at all disconnected with the higher spheres. It lives in all spheres but
knows mostly one sphere, ignorant of the other spheres on
which it turns its back. Thus, the soul becomes deprived of
the heavenly bliss and conscious of the troubles and limitations of life on the earth. It is not true that Adam was put
out of the Garden of Eden; he only turned his back on it,
and that was like an exile from heaven.

The souls of the seers, of saints and masters and
prophets, are conscious of the different spheres. It is, therefore, that they are connected with the worlds of angels and
jinns and with the spirit of God. The condition of the ignorant one becomes like a captive who is imprisoned on the
first floor of the house and has no access to the other floors
of the building, and of the seer is that he has access to all
the different floors of the building wherever he may wish to
dwell.

The secret of life is that every soul by its nature is an
akasha, an accommodation, and has in it an appetite; and
of all that it partakes, it creates of it a cover which surrounds
it as a shell, and the life of that shell becomes dependent
upon the same substance of which it is made. Therefore,
that shell becomes susceptible to all influences and subject
to the laws of that sphere from which it seeks its sustenance,
which means the sustenance of the shell.

The soul cannot see itself. It sees what is around it; it sees
that in which it is functioning, and so it enjoys the comforts
of that shell which is around it and experiences the pains
and discomforts which belong to that shell. In this way it

becomes an exile from its birthland, which is the being of God, which is the Divine Spirit, and seeks consciously or unconsciously once again the happiness and peace of home. God, therefore, is not the goal but the abode of the soul, its real self, its true being.

There are five spheres of which the soul is capable of being conscious. What are these spheres? These spheres are the different shells, each shell having its own world.

One, *nasut*, is a sphere which is commonly known as the physical sphere. How are the comforts and discomforts of this sphere experienced? By the medium of the physical body. And when there is something wrong with an organ of the body or of the senses, the soul becomes deprived of that particular experience that it would like to have of this physical sphere. This physical body, susceptible to all changes of climate, becomes dependent in its experience and expressions, thus making the soul dependent and limited. Therefore, all the riches that the world can give a man who is only conscious of this sphere, are limited. "God alone is rich and all souls living on earth are poor," says the Qur'an.

Malakut is the next sphere, the sphere of thought and imagination, where there is a greater freedom and less limitation than one experiences on the physical sphere. A man with thought and imagination can add to life that comfort and beauty which is lacking; and the more real his imagination becomes, the more conscious of that sphere of mind he proves to be. This sphere of mind is his world, not smaller than this world but much larger, a world which can accommodate all that the universe holds, and yet there would be a place in it to be filled.

Then there is a third sphere, *jabrut*, a sphere of the soul in which the soul is at home. This sphere the soul of an average man touches a moment. The man does not know where he was at that moment—he calls it abstraction. Do they not say when a person is not listening that he is not here? Every soul is lifted up to that sphere, even if it be for a moment, and by the light and life with which the soul is charged in that sphere, the soul is enabled to live on this earth the life full of struggles and difficulties. Nothing in the world could give man the strength that is needed to live a life on the earth if there were no blessing from heaven reaching him from time to time, of which he is so little aware.

The other two spheres are experienced in sleep, but they are not different spheres. They are only different because they are experienced in sleep. They are *malakut,* which is experienced in the dream, the world of mind, of thought and imagination; and *jabrut*, the state of deep slumber when even the mind is still, a sleep which makes the suffering patients free from pain, and for the prisoners, it frees them from their prisons. It is that state of sleep which takes away from the mind the load of worries and anxieties and removes from the body every exhaustion and tiredness, bringing to the mind and body such repose, rest and peace that after man has wakened from his deep sleep he feels comfortable, rested, invigorated, as if a new life has come to him. One would give anything in the world to have a deep sleep, though so few of us know its value. That state of *malakut* is reached in the wakeful state by the great thinkers, the great inventive minds, by the gifted artists, and is experienced by the seers and sages. It is to experience this that all the concentrations are given by spiritual teachers to the adepts. This fuller experience is then called *lahut.*

Hahut is another experience, a further stage which is experienced by souls who have attained the most high spiritual attainment which is called *samadhi* in Vedantic terms. In this experience a person is conscious of *jabrut*, and this state he brings about at will. For the sake of clarity they are explained as five spheres, but chiefly they are three spheres: *nasut*, the plane of the world of man; *malakut*, the world of the *jinn*; and *jabrut*, the angelic world.

Now there is a question, if a soul by rising to all these spheres becomes conscious of the *jinn* world and of the world of angels, or if it only sees within itself its self-made world of mind and the spheres of joy and peace in itself.

The answer is, yes, first it sees its own world by rising to the sphere called *malakut*. It experiences the joy and peace which belong to its own heart, and are of its own being. But that is one part of spiritual attainment. This part of attainment is the way of the Yogi.

The way in which the Sufi differs from the Yogi is in his expansion. And it is the two sides of the journey which are pictured by the two lines of the cross, the perpendicular and the horizontal line. The perpendicular line shows a progress straight within from *nasut* to *malakut*,[21] experiencing one's own world within oneself. But that which the horizontal line denotes is expansion.

The Sufi, therefore, tries to expand as he goes on progressing, for it is the largeness of the soul which will accommodate and in the end will become all-embracing. The man who will shut himself up from all men, however high spiritually he may be, he will not be free in *malakut*, in the higher sphere. He will have a wall around him, keeping away *jinn*s, and even angels when in the angelic world; and so his journey is exclusive. It is therefore that Sufism not only teaches concentration and meditation, which help to make oneself one-pointed, but also the love of God, which is expansion, the opening of the heart to all.

21

THERE ARISES a question, "What is the cause of the different stages of evolution that one sees in the world of variety?" The answer is that there are three principal causes. First is the heritage of the soul which it has brought from the angelic and from the *jinn* world. Second are the inherent qualities that a soul possesses, having received these from its parents and ancestors. Third is what the soul acquires after coming on earth. It is these three things which make what may be called individuality, which, in its result, culminates in a personality.

There are five principal stages of evolution recognized by the Sufis, named as five conditions of *nafs*, which means the ego. Every condition of the ego shows its pitch of evolution. As there are five elements and five notes recognized by the ancient musicians, so there are five egos, each showing a certain pitch.

Ammarah is the condition of the ego when it is blinded by passions. This shows the animal in man, and it is its fulness which is meant by the word "devil." Man, absorbed in his passions and emotions, is a kind of drunken person. He cannot always see the right, the right way in thinking, saying or doing. No doubt there are moments when every drunken person is sober, when he realizes his follies, but very often the longing for being intoxicated again sounds louder in his head, above the soft murmuring of his follies.

The second, *lawwama*, is the condition of mind which is full of thoughts, good and bad, over which the ego reigns, self-covering the truth. He has bitterness or spite against another, or he has his ways of getting all he desires cleverly, or he finds faults with others. He is worried about himself, anxious over his affairs, troubled about unimportant things. He struggles along through life, being confused by life itself. It is not that his passions and emotions trouble him. What troubles him are his own thoughts and his feelings.

Then there is the third, *mutmaina*, the person who, after his troubles and struggles through life, has arrived at a certain state of balance, of tranquillity, and by having arrived at this stage is beginning to enjoy to some degree the happiness which is within. He then concerns himself little with others for his own happiness. He then troubles little with others for their faults. He knows then how to throw off of himself the load of anxieties and worries that life in the world puts upon one's shoulders. He is then able to harmonize with others, to agree with others, and thus he brings about harmony in himself, in his atmosphere and spreads harmony around and about himself, thus harmonizing the whole atmosphere.

The fourth is *salima*, the person who has arrived at a point where though he be in the midst of the life of the world, yet he can rise above it. So life does not trouble him so much as it can trouble others. To him life is of no importance. Yet he fulfills his obligations, his duties in the world, in the same way as everyone else. He is the one of whom it may be said that he is in the world but is not of the world. His love embraces every soul that seeks refuge under his influence. His peace stills the mind of all he meets, regulating it to the same rhythm as his own. When the soul has arrived at that point, it becomes a blessing to itself and to others.

And there is the fifth condition, *alimah*, or God-conscious. His language becomes different. You cannot understand what his "no" means, what his "yes" means. You cannot very well comprehend the meaning of his smiles or of his tears. He may be sitting before you but he is not there. He may be speaking with you and yet communicating somewhere else. He may be among all and yet absent. You may think you hold him; he is not there. It is this soul which

122

proves the fulfilling of that purpose for which it came on earth.

The soul has not come on the earth to die the death of helplessness or to continually suffer pains and miseries. The soul has not come on earth that it may remain all through life perplexed and deluded. The purpose of the soul is that for which the whole creation has been busied, and it is the fulfilment of that purpose which is called God-consciousness.

* * *

Question: *If one of the reasons for the differences of the souls is caused by the different heritages from the angelic world, the question remains: what causes these differences?*

Answer: There are many mechanical reasons. For instance, if a person is bad natured it is because he has acquired that, or because his position makes him so, or because people make him so. But there is also a reason: because there is something wrong with him physically, though no one knows it. A person who is ill, at that time he will be irritable; a person who is tired, at that time he will be disagreeable, besides his bad nature. But the reason is a mechanical, physical reason, not a moral reason.

Therefore, there is a physical reason which can be seen from another point of view, which is vibrations. Every soul which starts from the divine sun, vibrates differently. What makes the notes of the piano different? Because of their difference in vibration. Only when they are harmonious, they give us great pleasure. Music can give us more pleasure even than spoken words. Therefore, the vibrations with which these souls start from the angelic world, they are of various kinds. That is the beginning which harmonizes, co-ordinates with all that comes in harmony with it. In this way by a vibratory law, souls in the first place attract and harmonize equal vibrations.

For instance, a person comes in the room, a strange person. You feel like welcoming that person, talking to him.

There is something attracting you to him. Another person comes in the room; he repels, his personality is repellent, if one thinks about it, even before that person has spoken one word. What is the cause?

To me, the one who always goes against the influence of the people, it is most amusing, most interesting to hear, "I do not like that person, I hate that person." That amuses me very much. They cannot understand the one whom Murshid stands. "If we cannot stand them, then he must stand them even less than us!" It amuses me very much. What is in that person that without his having talked to me, he is repellent so that I should have turned against him? What is it? It is the vibrations. When they do not harmonize with a person, that person feels a chill, even physically, mentally. He wants to run away.

If that is true, then the souls who have started from the angelic world are nothing but vibrations. As it is said in the Christian scriptures, the angels are playing on the harp. They have not got an earthly harp, they are harps themselves, they are music, they are vibrations themselves. And therefore, in accordance to that they attract what first comes to them. And they are directed to that because they are living vibrations; they are life itself.

Question: *Is it possible for children to be very inharmonious, and afterwards to become very harmonious?*

Answer: I have seen the contrary case, harmonious first, inharmonious afterwards. A child is very susceptible to vibrations. This must be remembered, that a person with excitable vibrations may come in the house and may not even see the children. When that person has gone, the children are more naughty; they are tuned to that pitch. For they take on the conditions of the atmosphere. A person full of depression may come into the home and the child will cry all night. Therefore, in the East there is a custom that for the first forty days the infant is not brought before anyone. Because at that time the infant is most susceptible, and it is kept in seclusion.

The Manifested Soul

Question: *When the soul comes to the angelic plane, is there already a tendency to differ?*

Answer: According to their own vibrations, they harmonize with those souls who are of the same harmony. For instance, there are different laws of harmony which I have given in *The Mysticism of Sound*.[22] I shall tell in short the two different kinds. The one law of vibrations and harmony is this: the similar element attracts the similar kind; that means a conceited person will be attracted to the conceited person, a humble person will be attracted to the humble, so good to the good, and bad to the bad. Just like the note *c*: if you play the note *c* on the piano in six or seven octaves, it will sound harmoniously because it is the same note. Wherever there is the same note, there is attraction.

There is another law: of contrast. And that law of contrast is such that sixty francs will be attracted to forty francs in order to make it a hundred. Ninety-nine will be attracted to one in order to make it complete. What one lacks, that something attracts. And very often, what happens? That which one lacks may have much less value in comparison to what one has, and yet one will pay anything for what one lacks. That is another law, and that is the law of contrast. Therefore, you will always find this when a person says, "Why does a serious person like this person seek a friendship with a very childish person?" But that is what he lacks. All day with a long face, what must he do? He must have something to give the other side. The monks and hermits, if they were brought to a theater, I am sure they would like it. It would benefit them. It is a pity they are not brought there.

Question: *At the beginning of all, the difference of vibration of souls may seem unjust. But if everything vibrated in the same way there would be no harmony.*

Answer: Rumi says, "Suppose we find the cause behind every cause; where shall we end?" Endless cause. There should be some end. The end is God. When we come to that end, there is no cause. God is the cause. That is the impression of the prophets and their inspiration. And therefore, they give the causes which are perhaps useful for the nourishment of the intellect, but at the same time they say that the cause of all causes is one, and that is God. Omar Khayyam treats that subject from the same point of view as St. Paul. He explains it more briefly.

Question: *What is the essential quality in a note, which makes it always the same though pronounced by different voices which have different vibration, different breath?*

Answer: Everything is in a circle. And where the circle is complete there comes the same thing again. For instance, infancy and old age. Youth is different, middle age is different. But there comes that condition of infancy in old age where innocence comes, and all bad feelings and wrong thoughts and pride and conceit, and all that is bad, acquired, becomes forgotten. And those childlike qualities with the helplessness of age begin to rise. And that is where the circle is complete.

For instance, there is the morning and the afternoon. But the circle becomes complete when it is again morning. In the same way there is a circle in the exhaling and inhaling. It is the completing of the circle which is the completing of the octave in music. Because before us there is a piano [a flat keyboard], but in reality it is not so, it comes round in a spiral.

There is the mechanical way, and the other way is natural. The mechanical is from mathematics; we can find which is *c* and from that we say, "This particular note is *c*." But there is a natural way; that is that the ancient people recognized the sounds of nature: the lightning, the thunder, the running of the water, the roaring of the sea, the sounds of animals and birds and human beings. And they made seven notes, discerning them from nature's tone. Then they saw the comparison [the interval] from natural sounds. Therefore, even till now in Sanskrit musical science there are notes which are nature's notes. And the tuning fork from which those notes can be compared and regulated is in nature, the sound of different animals; upon that *c, d, f* are based.

22

Every person shows from his earthly heritage a nature that divides men into four classes.

First is the idealist, who lives in the world for his ideal, with his ideal, a man of principles, intelligent, modest, moderate in everything, patient. He is a man with manner and principle, dreamy by nature or a deep thinker, a man of dignity, who guards his reputation as one would take care of a thin glass. His contact with the earth is like that of a bird, who builds its nest upon the tree, in the air, descends to the earth to pick up a grain when hungry, then flies off, even frightened by the flutter of the leaves. He lives on the earth because he is born on the earth, but in reality he lives in his thoughts. The earth and all that belongs to the earth is his need, not his want.

Second is the artist, the artist not necessarily by profession, but by nature. Artistic by temperament, he shows choice in his love, he is distinct in his likes and dislikes. Subtle, clever, witty, he observes conventions and yet is not bound by conventions. He notes everything and yet does not show himself fully, elusive by nature, yet tender and affectionate, fine and simple, sociable and yet detached. He shows the sign of a deer in the woods, who is one moment in one part of the forest and at another moment you will find him at quite a distance from there. One may think by coming in contact with him that one has got him, but at the next moment one will find him far from one's reach. This is the type of man of whom one might say, " I cannot understand him."

127

Third is the material man, material in his outlook, void of the love of beauty, concerned only with all he needs, clever but not wise. He lives all through life in the pursuit of earthly gain, ignorant of the beauty life can offer, looking from day to day with hope to that gain towards which he is working. In connection with this man one might say, "He is waiting for that day to come when his ship will arrive."

Fourth, there is a man with all desires, who enjoys his food and drink. What he knows is his bodily comfort, his momentary pleasures, his passing joy. The slave of passions and captive to the things of the earth, he is simple, disinterested in everything but himself. He belongs to no one, nor does anyone belong to him in reality. He is happy-go-lucky by nature, yet susceptible to depression and despair. It is in his case that one might say that he lives to eat.

These four different qualities belong to the body that the earth offers to the soul, the third and fourth qualities more than the first and second. It is by this that one can trace back the origin of this clay which the soul has adorned itself with and calls it "myself." This clay that has been passed through so many different conditions while being kneaded: through the mineral, through the vegetable, through the animal king-doms; and then of it was made the image of man. Verily, in man all is reflected, all that is on the earth and in heaven.

* * *

Question: *Will you please tell us if you include the mind in this inherited body? Is not idealism more in the mind than in the body?*

Answer: Yes, it is so. But at the same time the body could be so mundane that it could stand against idealism, if it did not allow the mind to express itself fully. It should be the body that is pliable to the ideal.

Question: *As the matter of the body changes every seven years, do we attract finer and finer qualities of matter as we develop spiritually?*

Answer: Certainly. Spiritual advancement has an etherealizing effect upon the body.

Question: *Is it possible that coarse food makes the body coarse, and then it cannot express anything but crude thoughts?*

Answer: Yes, it would be always attacking the mind's higher thoughts; there would be a conflict between the mind and the body.

Question: *What is the highest manifestation of the soul during his passage on the earth?*

Answer: Of course this question must be more fully explained before I could answer.

Question: *All souls start from the angelic plane pure of faults, because in the angelic plane there is no impurity and wickedness, and all is perfection, is it not so?*

Answer: It is not so. There is purity, there is no wickedness, but there is no perfection. There is only one perfection and that is God. There cannot be perfection where there is duality. Where there are two, there is no perfection, there is only a glimpse of perfection. God only is perfect when he rises above "one." Even "one" limits him.

Question: *Is it then on earth that the soul learns all the imperfections which every human being shows, or has he learned this on the jinn plane from the spirits returning from the earth, which he meets when coming down to earth?*

Answer: Imperfection is not learned. Imperfection is a state of being; it is limitation which is imperfection. Limitation is the condition of life. If God is perfect, all others are imperfect; however great, strong, mighty, they are all imperfect. All goes towards perfection. This whole manifestation is made that we all go towards perfection. The interest of life is going towards perfection. If we were born perfect, there would be no joy in life, no interest. The whole beauty we enjoy in our imperfection, we admire something which is greater. If there were nothing to look up to, there would be no purpose to live for. Therefore, one must not make a great haste in spiritual attainment; it is too bad to be too impatient.

Question: *Do these four types correspond with the elements?*

Answer: We can make them correspond. They do not necessarily. One shows the earthly qualities, the other water qualities, the third the air element, and the fourth ether.

Question: *Are there differences in these four types as to man and woman?*

Answer: No, they are the same for man and woman.

Question: *Is it possible to change that type?*

Answer: All is subject to change. One could change entirely from one type to another. Yes, even such a vast distance as there is between saint and sinner can be changed. For I have always been unwilling to admit it when a person says, "This person behaved very wickedly last month." And if that person is brought to me, I will say, "It was last month; that is gone." It may not be so today; even if he were wicked yesterday, today there is a hope.

An accusation of last month has no claims for me today. The reason is that man by nature is good. Goodness is his very self, his very being. Badness is only a cloud over him. And the cloud is not such a thing which is pinned; it is the ever-floating game: it is sometimes here, sometimes it has moved. Do the clouds remain in the same position? So badness, evil, does not remain. Just as a cloud that passes, it comes and goes. And if we trust in the goodness of man, there may be a thousand clouds of wickedness, and they may disappear one day. Our very trust will break it.

For the depth of every soul is good. And it is the belief in this doctrine which can be the reason of the belief in the goodness of God. God cannot be good if man can always be wicked, for the origin of man is in God. As God is good, so man is good; wickedness is a passing phase.

Question: *Will you please tell us what determines the choice of the four qualities that the earth offers to the soul?*

Answer: Really speaking, these four distinct qualities are also a speculation of the human mind, as the human mind distinguishes these four qualities. But in the point of fact, there are myriads of qualities. Every quality has its origin in the heritage. And it is a kind of mixture of different qualities, a kind of solution, just like a medicine is made of different drugs and herbs, and so one prescription is not like another prescription. And so every person has a peculiar personality, has his peculiar qualities. And every person is unique in his way. And in this lies the secret of the oneness of God. That not only is God one, but man is one; he is one, unlike anyone else. There God proves that God is one.

Question: *Then everyone has everything in him, but in different degrees?*

Answer: Yes, but it is not necessary to be discouraged or disappointed in life, because man has the key to his own life in his hand, if he only knew. And it is absurd to say, " I have not got this." There is nothing in this world that he has not got, either a good quality or a bad quality. Man has everything. His denial of having it makes him weak and ignorant of that key which he has. And the most psychological secret is this: that what one thinks desirable, best attainable, one must affirm, and say one has that in oneself. And what is undesirable one must deny: "It does not belong to me." That is the key.

Question: *Is our standard of good and bad by our vanity?*

Answer: Not our standard, but vanity itself is a power behind every impulse which leads man to good or bad. It is the living spark of the ego.

23

THE QUESTION, "Why do souls come on earth? Why has this creation taken place, What is the purpose of this manifestation?" may be answered in one word: satisfaction; for the satisfaction of God. Why is God not satisfied without it? Because God is the only being, and the nature of being is to become conscious of one's being. And this consciousness experiences life through various channels, names and forms; and through man this consciousness of being reaches its culmination.

Plainly speaking, through man God experiences life to its highest perfection. If anyone asked, "Then what is man's duty, if that be the purpose?" the answer is that his sacred duty is to attain to that perfect consciousness which is his *dharma*, his true religion. In order to perform this duty he will have to struggle with himself, he will have to go through sufferings and pains, he will have many tests and trials to go through, and by making many sacrifices and practicing renunciation, he will attain that consciousness which is God-consciousness, in which resides all perfection. But why must man suffer and sacrifice for God? At the end of his suffering and sacrifice he will find that though he began to do so for God, in the end it turned out to be all for himself. It is the foolishly selfish who are selfish, and the wisely selfish who prove to be selfless.

Now the question, "How may this consciousness be attained?" It is to be attained by self-realization. First man must analyze of what he is composed. He is composed of spirit and matter. He constitutes in himself the animal world, the mineral world, the vegetable world, the *jinn* and the angel, and it is his work to balance it, knowing that neither has he been created to be as spiritual as an angel nor has he been made to be as material as an animal. And when he strikes the happy medium, he will certainly tread the path which is meant for a human being to tread, the path which leads straight to the goal. "Strait is the gate and narrow is the way."[23] Narrow is the way because any steps taken on either side will lead to some other street.

Balance is the keynote of spiritual attainment. In order to attain to God-consciousness, the first condition is to make God a reality, that he no longer is an imagination. No sooner is the God-ideal brought to life, than the worshiper of God turns into truth. There is no greater religion than truth. Then truth no longer is his seeking; then the truth becomes his being and in the light of that absolute truth he finds all knowledge.

No question remains unanswered. That continual question that arises in the heart of man, "Why?" then becomes nonexistent, for with every "Why?" rises its answer the moment one has become the owner of the house. For it is the difficulty of the stranger to find any room in the house, not the one who lives in it. He knows about the whole house. What is rooted out in the quest of truth is the ignorance that is entirely removed from one's heart, and the outlook becomes wide, as wide as the eye of God. Therein is born the divine spirit, the spirit which is called divinity.

* * *

Question: *Is it possible for every soul to attain God-consciousness?*

Answer: It is born for it. Every soul is born for it.

Question: *Self-consciousness is higher than God-consciousness; how is that?*

Answer: The surface of the true self of all is God, but the depth of everyone's true self is the Self. When I said "Self

134

consciousness," I meant the Self.

Question: *That is why that by God-realization one realizes oneself?*

Answer: Yes.

Question: *Does the rest of the manifestation reach that stage as human beings do?*

Answer: No. But it touches that stage without being conscious.

Question: *For the one who does not reach self-realization in his life on earth, does he reach it in the hereafter? Is here better?*

Answer: Perhaps more easily then, but at the same time one must try and do today what one can do today rather than leaving it today. Nothing that one really values will one put off till tomorrow. One puts it off because one does not value it enough.

Question: *Is it right to say that God becomes conscious of his own consciousness through man?*

Answer: Yes, man becomes the best instrument for God's own purpose. There is a certain satisfaction of having put it into an objective form and on another plane. It is here. By taking part in the play which was given here [*Una*24], you produced before me that which I had made up in my mind. How could you accomplish it? You had to accomplish it by putting yourself away, you had to be different. That is the secret of the whole thing. When you are no more yourself— what you had thought yourself to be—that is the secret.

The journey is three steps, if one only knows how to accomplish it. Annihilation, which is such a frightening word, is nothing but this, the same thing: When in the play you came in a different form, that was the annihilation of the first self and appearance, of the name and that form, by adorning yourself with another name and appearance. But that annihilation never kills a person; it is only a continuation.

Question: *What are the three steps of the path of annihilation?*

Answer: These are three steps of the path of annihilation: one step is in the ideal of form, and the other is in the ideal of name, and the third is in the nameless and formless, which in Sufi terms are *fana-fi-Sheikh, fana-fi-Rassul, fana-fi-Allah*.

24

HAS THE WORLD of the *jinn* many worlds, as there are planets in our universe? Yes, many, and as different from one another as the planets in our universe are different, yet not so far apart as in our universe, not so out of communication as in our universe.

Is the heaven of the angels created on the same model? Yes, but it is on the model of the heaven of the angels that our universe has been molded and that of the *jinn*.

What is the life there? What is it like? It is difficult to explain and difficult to put in words. But for an example, one might see the difference in the life of the birds which can fly over seas and forests and fly about over hills and dales, and feel in tune with nature and express their joy in song. Then there are the deer in the woods, dwelling in the caves of the mountains, drinking water at the natural springs, moving about in the open spaces, looking at the horizon from morning till evening, the sun their time-keeper and the moon serving as their torch. And then imagine our lives, the lives of human beings in crowded cities, days in the factories and nights indoors, away from God, away from nature, even away from self, fully absorbed in the struggle of life, an ever increasing struggle, and there is no end to it. There is the picture before us to imagine what life the angels live in the highest heavens, what life the *jinns* have in the middle heaven and to compare them with our life as human beings in our universe.

Are there suns, are there moons in their worlds as we have in ours? Yes, this outer solar system is the reflection of the inner solar system. What difference is there between the conception of time that we have and the idea of time which is there? There is an incomparable difference. No words will give the exact idea of the comparison between time, but for the sake of convenience, let us say our year is the *jinn*'s hour and the moment of the angel. Are there angels and *jinns* of longer and shorter lives just as men on earth? Certainly there are, but the time of their life is not to be compared with that of human beings.

Are there differences between the *jinns* and between the angels, as among men of different sorts? Indeed there are, but among the *jinns* not so many differences as among men, and still less among the angels.

What about the time that every soul spends in the heaven of the angels and the heaven of the *jinns*? The speed of every soul is different; it is according to the speed with which they manifest—it is a different dimension. The difference of speed is the way traveling on the earth, traveling in the water, and journeying through the air are different. The difference of speed between different souls may be likened to one child advancing in his thought so that he may learn in ten years something which another one has not learned in a hundred years of life on earth. Nevertheless, as they say: "Slowly and surely." The souls with a balance and rhythm through their manifestation learn and experience much more than by a rapid run through the heavens.

* * *

Question: *Do the* jinn *and angelic worlds occupy what we would call the same space as our world and pervade it?*

Answer: The question of the space is a difficult one to answer very well in words; the reason is that because of the space which we are accustomed to know as space, we can only think of any other space in the same way as the space we are accustomed to. For instance, there is so little said about the space which is in the iris, in the pupil of the eye, so small and yet so vastly accommodating. If that space is accommodating, that little space of the eye, so little if we measure it according to our idea of space, what is the explanation of that space accommodation? If this is so accommodating that thousands of miles can come in and it can accommodate, then there is another space which is different from this space. And when this idea has become clear to man, then before him the vision of the heavens is open.

A Chinese philosopher, while answering the question, "What is soul like?" said, "Like the iris, the pupil of the eye," which means that it is an accommodation, it accommodates. It is a space itself. And think of the heart. If there were a thousand universes it would accommodate them, it is so large. Although every person knows the name of the heart, he cannot realize what the heart is. If he only knew it, he would say as the mystic Nizam has said, "What is this earth and the whole cosmos? If the doors of the heart were open, the heart would prove larger than the whole universe."[25] And what little one can say is by showing the picture of the cross, that there is a horizontal space, and then there is the other kind of space, which can be pictured as a perpendicular line. It is not the same space, it is quite a different space. And it is to explain that space the mystics and the seers have used the word "within"; to explain this space they have used the word "without."

Question: *Can an illuminated soul be conscious of all the past events in the evolution of man?*

Answer: To some extent. I would ask, "This eye, which is so accommodating, does it collect within itself all that it sees?" Besides, the mind which has the most wonderful source of record, which is memory, does it always remember all that it sees and experiences through life? No, only certain things which have made a deeper impression upon it. If we remembered all the faces we have seen after one trip to Paris, I do not know where a person would be! And if we remember all things, all the good and bad words that people have said, insults and bitterness, and foolish and crazy things, where would we be at the end?

139

The human being, his mind, his body and his health—it all depends upon all he takes in and then puts out. If it were not so, he would not live. He takes its essence and then it is all thrown away. Therefore, if one takes from the angelic world or from the *jinn* world, it is the essence of experience. If not, how would one live, how would one digest?

But there is another thing. I think that person must not be very much complimented, the person who remembers every good and bad thing of the past. He ought to be pitied. Because he must have many experiences of great remorse; it would only create bitterness in him. It is the greatest relief to forget. It is like bathing in the Ganges. That is the meaning of being purified of the past. The present has so many beautiful things to offer us if we opened ourselves to the beauty that we do not need to look for beauty in the past. Beauty is always there—only we have to open our heart to it—ever new and ever fresh.

Question: *Are the* jinns *conscious of the angels, or the angels conscious of the* jinns?

Answer: Not all; as all human beings are not conscious of the angels and *jinns*, so the *jinns* are not conscious of the angels. But some are conscious.

Question: *Does the time a soul remains in the angelic or* jinn *heaven depend on its earthly life?*

Answer: I have not come yet to that subject, because this subject will be given in the return journey.

Question: *To what extent is the difference of the speed of a soul a difference from his past?*

Answer: The difference in each heaven is incomparable. The difference of a journey in each heaven is incomparable because of the difference of speed. The speed is much quicker in the higher world compared with the lower world, quickest in the heaven of the angels.

Question: *When you compare two souls together in the same sphere?*

Answer: There can be a very great difference, an immense difference. The difference among the angels may be of thousands of years.

Question: *I do not know what is meant by the fourth dimension.*

Answer: I use the word dimension in the difference of the space. When I say, "It is a different dimension," then I mean a space, the character of which is different. If I say "different dimension," this is the accommodation which is in the space. For instance, in the iris is a different dimension. If we call this earthly sphere one dimension, and the sphere of the *jinn* a second, the sphere of the angel the third, then the sphere of God is the fourth. So if not in the meaning of length, breadth and height, then it is the fourth which is being sought after.

Question: *Is there a book we might study to understand more about this different dimension?*

Answer: The *Arabian Nights* is a very good book to study. After having studied mysticism, then reading the *Arabian Nights*, it would throw quite a different light upon it because the whole book is written in an allegorical language. After having studied mysticism, then it explains the whole mysticism. In every story there is some mystical secret hidden. Because those who realized those secrets, if they would have given them in the scriptures, then people would have troubled them very much. Only just here and there a word; that after having found out that it is a key. If the scriptures would have given this, there would have been a revolution.

Question: *Is the* Arabian Nights *written by Sufis?*

Answer: Yes, it is Sufi novel. There is another Sufi novel. There are two ways of expressing: one in legend, another in poetry.[26] That came from the Persians; the Arabs gave it in legends, in novels.

25

THE WORD *akasha* in the language of the Hindus is expressive of a meaning that explains its object. *Akasha* means accommodation, not necessarily the sky, although the sky is an accommodation. And on the model of *akasha* the whole creation has been based.

The organs of the senses—the ears, the eyes, the nostrils, the mouth—all are different aspects of *akasha* and so is the human body constructed. And the purpose of this construction can be found in its own nature; as the purpose of the ears is found in hearing, of the nostrils in breathing, of the eyes in seeing, so is the purpose of the whole body. The purpose of the body is to experience life fully. For the intelligence, the body becomes a vehicle by which the intelligence is enabled to experience life fully.

In order to make sound more audible, people build domes and places where the sound becomes more audible, where resonance is produced and the voice and words become more clear. So the construction of the body is made to make all that is perceptible clear, for by nature the body is the vehicle of the intelligence or of the soul by which it experiences life fully. But as man has lived for generations an increasing life of artificiality, he has moved further and further from nature. Therefore, this vehicle, which was made a perfect instrument to experience life fully, has become more and more incapable of attaining that object. It is this incapability of experiencing life fully and that innate desire for the experience of life which makes the soul strive for spiritual attainment.

What man does not know, he thinks does not exist. In

this is to be found the reason for materialism. But the tendency towards spiritual realization remains there, as an innate desire, which is consciously or unconsciously felt by every soul, whether spiritual or material. It is therefore that a material person has a silent craving in his heart to probe the depth of the spiritual ideal which he disowns.

The work of the senses is to experience taste, smell, touch, to hear and to see. But besides this, the inner sense is one sense. It is by experiencing through different organs of the senses that one sense becomes many senses. It is the same sense which hears, sees, smells, tastes and feels touch, but because it experiences life through different organs, the one sense is divided into five senses. The depth of that sense, which is the inner sense, is more subtle than a person can imagine. When that sense finds a free expression, it does not only experience life more keenly by the help of the organs of the senses, but it becomes independent of the organs of the senses. It penetrates life deeply, and as Kabir says, "It sees without eyes and hears without ears."[27] The reason is this: that all that exists is contained in an accommodation, in the *akasha*. And by being in the *akasha* the nature of all things is revealed. Plainly speaking, there is nothing in this world which does not speak. Every thing and every being is continually calling out its nature, its character and its secret. And the more the inner sense is open, the more it becomes capable of hearing the voice of all things. In every person this sense is for the greater part hidden, buried, and its being buried gives it discomfort, for it is something which is living—the only living being there is. The idea of the "lost word" has its secret in this.[28] When once this inner sense has broken the walls around it which keep it closed, it breathes freedom, and that happiness, which is the soul's own property, the soul attains.

Every discomfort, from whatever source it comes, comes from the lack of understanding. The more the inner sense is covered, the more it finds itself in obscurity. It is therefore that the sign of the enlightened soul is that readiness to understand. Therefore, they are easy to reconcile with.

When a person can understand himself better, he can make another person understand better also. But when a person is perplexed himself, he, instead of making another person understand, confuses him. In this way differences are produced.

* * *

Question: *Is every unhappiness a material phenomenon?*

Answer: Yes. The greatest unhappiness that a person feels comes from lack of mastery. This unhappiness comes when, although knowing mastery, man cannot practice that which he knows. Sadness comes from limitation, limitation in different forms: lack of perception, lack of power over one-self, or over one's condition and the lack of that substance which is happiness itself, which is love.

Question: *If a person has mastery, is he still made unhappy by the unhappiness of others?*

Answer: There is often a lack of understanding, though there may be love, and often a lack of love, though no lack of understanding. There may be love and understanding and yet a lack of power. Unhappiness comes always from limitation.

Question: *Can there be love without understanding?*

Answer: If love has reached perfection, it will obtain all these three powers. When love becomes power, love becomes understanding. The nature of love is as the nature of water hidden in the depth of the earth. If one digs but does not dig deep enough, one finds mud, not water. When one digs deep enough, one finds water. Many lose patience, trust and hope; they have touched the mud and not reached the water. But when they dig deep enough, they find pure water.

Question: *If a person can be happy by the power of his soul, this means that he can wipe out his sins. But how is it with the debt he has to pay sooner or later?*

Answer: There is a board and the board comes to an end after 100 years. It wears out gradually, but if you know how to end it, you may put it in the fire and finish it in one moment. Or by surrounding it with some chemical substance you may preserve it for a very long time. So with sins; all that has been made can be destroyed. If one individual has the power of destroying, another has the power of creating. Creating is more difficult than destroying. A great Sufi saint, on hearing from his mureeds problems of sin and virtue, reward and virtue, said, "My mureeds, do not worry over problems of sin and virtue. They are things which man makes."

The difficulty is that man lives so much in the outer life, he thinks he can destroy a table or a chair because he holds it in his hand, but what he holds in thought and feeling, he is not master, but slave of. But if he can learn to be master of his feeling, he can destroy what he wishes.

26

THE ORGANS of the senses are the *akashas* or accommodations of grosser and finer nature. The finer the organ, the more perceptive it is; grossness takes away from the organ its power of perception. This shows that the body may be likened to a glass house made of mirrors. In the Persian language, the poets have called the body *aina khana*, meaning the temple of mirrors.

The eye stands as a mirror before all that is visible. It reflects all that it sees. The ears are the accommodation for the re-echo of every sound that falls upon them. In other words, the ears are the mirror of every sound. The senses of touch and of taste are grosser in comparison to the senses of sight and hearing. At the same time their nature is the same. All the different savors—sweet, sour, salt, and the feeling of warm and cold are perceived by them, and these savors and sensations stand as mirrors in which taste and touch are reflected. Therefore, as in a mirror one sees oneself reflected, so this body stands as a mirror in which every experience of the outer life is reflected and is made clear. If the mirror is dusty, it does not show the image clearly; so the experience of life is not clear when the body is not looked after according to the spiritual point of view.

The Sufis say that the body is the temple of God but the right interpretation of this saying is that the body is made to be the temple of God; a temple cannot be called a temple of God if God is not brought and placed there. So it is natural when a soul feels downhearted or depressed that there is something wrong with the vehicle. When the writer wishes to work and the pen is not in order, it annoys him;

there is nothing the matter with the writer, it is the pen which is not right. No discomfort comes from the soul; the soul is happy by nature, the soul is happiness itself. It becomes unhappy when something is the matter with its vehicle, which is its instrument, its tool with which to experience life. Care of the body, therefore, is the first and the most important principle of religion. Piety, without this thought, is of little significance.

The soul manifests in this world in order that it may experience the different phases of the manifestation and yet may not lose its way and be lost, but may attain its original freedom in addition to the experience and knowledge it has gained in this world. The different exercises that the Sufis and Yogis do in order to enable the mind and body to experience life more fully, exercises such as fasting, poses, postures, movement, all these things help to train the body that it may become a fitting vehicle for the experience of life.

Wonder-working such as psychometry, feeling the atmosphere of places, of objects, of people, all this comes when the body also is prepared for it. A person may be intelligent, clever, learned, good or pious, and yet his sense of perception may not be fully awake. It must be remembered as the first principle of life that manifestation was destined for a keener observation of life within and without.

* * *

Question: *If the past can be destroyed, what happens to the* akashic *records?*

Answer: What is once created, manifests and goes on manifesting. It requires a tremendous power to destroy what one has created, but the idea of the mystic is hidden in the word "annihilation," which is not generally understood. Annihilation is really the art of the mystic. Shiva is called the destroyer; his power is considered greater than that of Brahma, the Creator. This subject takes man into one of the greatest of mysteries. If there were no means of destroying, then the inharmonious elements would consume the whole creation. By means of destruction, creation is restored, but

148

one must know what to destroy. A Persian verse says, "The master-mind is that which knows what to destroy and what to restore." The plants and trees have bugs and germs. These may be destroyed and the plant may be better. So in the character of man, in his mind and thought, are things that may be destroyed. Many people hold the thought of illness fast for many years, and in spite of many remedies, they are still ill. Healing is the way of destroying these thoughts. True healing is the destruction of these thoughts.

Question: *As the whole life is based on destroying, and the end, the fulfilment of all creation, will be destroying, what is meant by the Buddhistic law "not to destroy?" Why is this law not in this form in other religions? Is "not to destroy" an incomplete expression of a law? What is the real meaning of that law and how should it be in its more balanced expression?*

Answer: The idea of the Buddhist in not to destroy is that which should be maintained should be protected. The people who are very destructive are destroying things which should be protected and preserved. So kindness and love are taught to the people. They are taught to feel the pain of others, to sympathize with their sufferings. But one must remember that often by destroying one gives happiness. There are things which must be destroyed in order to produce happiness. There are sometimes thoughts, imaginations, feelings and impressions which must be destroyed. The master-mind knows clearly what to destroy and what to protect. For to the master-mind the whole world becomes a kind of garden, and as the gardener knows what to destroy and what to keep, so the master-mind knows what is to be protected and what is to be destroyed.

27

As THERE ARE different organs of the senses, so there are the centers of inner perception. The Sufis have called the five centers of inner perception by the terms *arsh, kursi, lauh, qalam, arsh-ul-azam*. These centers denote seats of intuitive faculties.

Two among these centers are of great importance: the heart and the head. If the Sufi training differs from that of the Yogis, it is in training both these centers together, by which the Sufi produces balance. The head without the heart shows dry intellect; the heart without the head represents an unbalanced condition. The balance is the use of both these faculties. The whole Sufi training is based on this principle.

The centers may be likened to the space that one finds in the apple. It is an *akasha*, an accommodation, where not only smell, touch, seeing and hearing are perceived, but even the thought and feeling of another is perceived, the condition in the atmosphere is perceived, the pleasure and displeasure of one's fellow man is perceived. And if the sense of perception is keener, then even the past, present and future can be perceived. When man does not perceive it, by this it does not mean that it is foreign to man's nature. It only means the soul is not wakened to that perception.

The absence of such fine perception naturally causes depression and confusion, for the soul longs for a keener perception and feels confused and at times agitated owing to the lack of a fuller perception, as a person who is blind feels nervous, agitated, because the inner longing is to see, and when the organ of sight fails one, one becomes agitated.

This generally is the cause hidden in many souls who feel uncomfortable, and the life we live, a life of artificiality, works against it. We do not need to read the ancient traditions to find out the truth about it. Today the people who live a less artificial life, a more simple life, a life [based] in nature, their intuitive faculties are more keen and they show a greater happiness.

These centers become blocked by certain foods, by living a more materialistic life. These centers are located in such places as there are some plants in the caves of the mountains where the sun does not reach, where the air cannot touch, and it is difficult for the plants to live there. And so it is with the centers of perception. The physical body is nourished by food but these centers remain without any nourishment. The physical body is made of matter, its sustenance is matter. But the centers of perception, located in the physical body where no nourishment can reach, can be reached by that which is drawn in through the breath, the fine substance which is not even visible. In the language of the mystics it is called *nur*, which is light.

The body not only wants food but also breath, in other words vibration, and that vibration is given to it by the repetition of sacred words. The sounds and vowels and the composition of the sacred words is chemical and it is this chemistry which was called by the ancient philosophers *chemia* or *alchemia*.[29]

These centers are the *akashas* or domes where every sound has its re-echo, and the re-echo, once produced in this *akasha*, reaches all other *akashas* which exist within and without. Therefore, the repetition of a sacred word has not only to do with oneself and one's life, but it spreads and rises higher than we can imagine and wider than man can perceive. Verily, every movement has its influence upon every atom of the universe; every action sets to movement every atom of the universe.

* * *

Question: *As the Sufi training differs from that of the Yogis in training both centers of heart and head together, there must be two ways of the Yogi training, i.e. training the heart more than the head and training the head more than the heart. Is this right? Will you tell us more about it?*

Answer: The Yogis of ancient times had one training only, the training of the head center to make the sight keen and the perception deep, but the training of the heart is the Sufi method. Among the Yogis came, from the time of Krishna, the training of *bhakti*. The Sufi has always considered that the training of head and heart gives balance in life.

If one visits in India places of the great Yogis and of the great Sufis, the atmosphere and the impression that one gets in the presence of the Yogi is very strong; the impression is that everything is worthless and nothing is worthwhile in life. Only one thing they desire, and that is to get away from it, and by getting away from it, to get above it. This makes one feel that one does not wish to remain one moment in this world, one wants to go to the caves and forests and to pass one's whole life in the eternal peace, the only true bliss and happiness there is. Then there is the feeling in the presence of the Yogi as if nothing exists, not even trees, plants, birds. The overwhelming influence of the Yogi is such that the person feels for the moment that he is blind and deaf to the whole world. He only feels the one eternal being, all else is nonexistent for him, and in his presence you may even come to the point where you do not know any existence at all.

In the presence of the Sufi you feel the atmosphere of love, kindness, affection, service, sociability, friendliness—because the central theme of the Sufi is God, his beloved. So he lives in the presence of his beloved, and love he considers as life. So in his presence you have the feeling of the fulness of joy and of the fragrance of roses, of incense bringing ecstasy with the joy. Many in disappointment, heartbroken and in trouble, go into the presence of the Sufi and from his word, his glance, his silence, his atmosphere, get encouraged to fight on, courage to look forward to life; if it is not good now, it will be better tomorrow; if he does not understand now, he will tomorrow. That which he cannot attain now, tomorrow will be attainable.

A Sufi always has hope, because while the idea of the Yogi begins with the object to lose his self and to live in the perfection of God, the Sufi begins his journey to perfection in the human soul first, and in this the Sufi considers the fulfilment of coming upon earth. After accomplishing this, the other thing which the Yogi strives for does not come with such difficulty. The Sufi can then easily attain that ideal, which is one step further. In this way the Sufi fulfills the first step, to experience the perfection of the human soul. A second step is to learn the perfection of the being of God.

To one, the Yogi part is more akin, but as far as I see, I think that to many the part of the Sufi appeals most. Imagine if all had to leave the world and go to the caves and the forests in order to become wise, then what would the world be without any of the wise? The power of the Yogi is such that their presence is an intoxication. To the Indian temperament the Yogi method appeals much. *Vairagya* is very dear to the people of India. The very presence of the Yogi convinces many of the futility of life.

Question: *What do you mean by saying that breath gives food and breath to the centers?*

Answer: Food and breath both: food taken into the breath and breath also in a symbolical sense, breath created by the power of vibration. Just as in an engine, steam is necessary as well as the engineer, so in the working of the centers two things are necessary: nourishment of finer food inhaled through the breath and vibrations of finer motions created by the repetition of a certain word. This word sets certain atoms into motion so they come to life again.

Question: *What is the proportional value of the sacred words spoken in the silence?*

Answer: The mind has its own vibration. A person, for instance in a chaotic state of mind, comes into your presence and you feel it at once. Therefore, thought has its vibration, but thought and word together make the vibration more perfect and more powerful.

28

W HEN ONCE the inner sense has become keen, it shows its development first by working through the organs of the senses. The vision becomes clear, hearing becomes clearer, the sense of touch felt more keenly, the sense of taste clearer, the sense of smell also. Therefore, among those who tread the mystical path, one finds many who are sensitive and become more sensitive as they develop spiritually. As the standard of normal health known by the average person is much beneath the mystical ideal, often to the uninitiated the sensitiveness of a person of mystical temperament might seem peculiar. At the same time when it is developed by spiritual training, the sensitiveness is under control. This manifests as the first thing in the life of a seer.

The body which covers the soul keeps it blind by depriving it of its freedom of expression in keener perception. It is like a captivity for the soul. When the centers in the body are awakened and at work, then the soul experiences life more clearly, and naturally clouds, which give depression, clear away. The soul begins to look forward to life with hope and trust, and with courage, and thus attains that power and understanding which is needed to struggle through life.

When a little more advanced, the intelligence begins to see through the eyes what every eye cannot see; the finer forces of nature manifest in colors and forms. There are many who talk much about this and some who know but say little, for they do not see wisdom in telling about something which the other person standing next to them does not see. And of those who speak much about seeing many things which others do not see, there is hardly one among them who really sees.

There is no doubt that as the sight becomes keen, first the finer colors of different elements working in nature manifest to view. Next, the atmosphere that is created around man, which is composed of semi-material atoms, becomes manifest to one's eyes. This is what is called the aura. The different colors of the aura denote the meaning of it, for there is nothing in this world which is without meaning. The one who pursues the meaning of life in all its aspects hears again in the end the word which was once lost for him.[30]

No doubt the life of a sensitive person becomes difficult, especially when he has to live amidst the crowd. It is therefore that the Brahmins lived an exclusive life, which has been criticized now by some who do not know the meaning of it. Different practices of breathing become a great help in training the mind and body both, to make them more perceptive in order that they may become fitting vehicles to fulfil the purpose of life.

29

THE MIND is not necessarily the brain. Mind is a capacity, an *akasha*, which contains all the experiences we make in life. It has all the impressions we gain through our five senses. It is not in the body, it is around the body. But the centers of perception reflect every thought and feeling, and thus man feels that his mind is within him. In point of fact, the body is in the mind, within the mind, not the mind within the body. As the eye sees an object before it and reflects it, so the centers of perception reflect every thought and feeling. For instance, the sensation of joy or depression one feels in the center called the solar plexus. But it does not mean that joy or depression is there, but that this center is sensitive to experience it.

The mind, for the sake of convenience, may be called a substance which is not necessarily matter, a substance quite different from matter in its nature and character. There are objects which give more resonance and there are other objects which respond less to sound. There are sonorous objects, such as metals of different kinds, which produce sound clearly, and then stone and solid wood, which do not respond to sound. Such is the difference between mind and body.

The mind is a better vehicle for the intelligence than the body. Therefore, though the mind experiences life even through the material organs of the senses, still the mind is more perceptive and can experience life and its different aspects standing aside from the body. In other words, the mind can see for itself, it can hear, even without the eyes and the ears, for the mind has its own eyes and ears.

Though the mind needs the physical eyes and ears to see and hear, still there are things which the physical eyes cannot see and the physical ears cannot hear—the mind sees and hears them. The more independent the mind is made of the outer senses, the more freely the mind perceives life and becomes capable of using the outer senses, the organs of the senses, to their best advantage.

The question, "Has the mind a form?" may be answered, yes, the mind has the same form with which the soul is most impressed. The question, "What form is there with which the soul is most impressed?" may be answered, one's own form. That is why when man says "I," he identifies himself with the form which is most impressed upon his mind and that is his own.

But the mind is a world in itself, a magic world, a world which can be more easily changed, more quickly altered compared with the physical form. The phenomenon of the mind is so great, and such wonders can be performed if one had the key of the mind in one's hand. The difficulty is that man becomes so fixed in his physical body that he hardly realizes that he has a mind. What man knows of himself is of the body, though the mind, which is called *mana* in Sanskrit, is at the root of the word "man."

* * *

Question: *Is the form of mind character?*

Answer: No, the soul, the spirit of man is his character. The form of the mind is what the mind thinks about, and generally it thinks about the body which is attached to it. So, when anything is wrong with the body, the mind feels, "I am ill," while the pain and discomfort is not in the mind, it is in the body. It is reflected back in the mind. The mind has power to hold everything in its memory; so even if the body is cured by medicine, if the mind still holds the thought of pain, the body cannot give up the illness.

The greatest difficulty in the spiritual path is to remove the false self from the intelligence; it stands in the way of the soul. It strives for all that pertains to the false self. So the soul is kept busy with something, which in the end is nothing, and cannot see beyond it.

Question: *What is the key of the mind?*

Answer: The key of the mind is to open the house of the mind, to open all the doors and cupboards and see what is hidden, what is valuable, what is worth keeping, and what should be put out. The soul is like the crown-prince; he does not know the secrets of his kingdom, he knows he is the crown-prince and once he gets the key he enters into possession. His kingdom is then before him.

Question: *Do you mean to say that the key to the mind is the wish that goes out for morality, in other words that it lies in the heart?*

Answer: No. The key to the mind is the knowledge of life. There is only one real knowledge; it is learned in one moment if one remembers. But the nature of life is such that we forget. The key to the mind is the knowledge of life; in other words it is the psychology of life. Very rarely is there a person who knows the psychology of life profoundly. Man has the faculty of knowing, but is so absorbed in life that he does not give time to learn the psychology of life, which is more precious than anything in the world.

By psychology I mean if, before uttering a word, a man would think what effect upon the atmosphere, upon the person, upon the whole of life it would have. Every word is a materialization of thought; it has a dynamic power. If one were to think, one would find every little thought, every little feeling, every little movement one makes, even a little smile or a little frown, such a little thing, but if one knew the effect of every cause before bringing that cause to thought, speech or action, one would become wise. Generally, man does all mechanically, influenced by the conditions of the time. Anger or downheartedness did it, not he, but his broken spirit did it, as every man lives a life without control, in other words, without mastery.

What we gain in spiritual knowledge is to gain mastery, to learn what consequences our actions will bring. A man cannot be perfect in this knowledge, all souls have their limitations, but it is something to strive after. In this is the fulfilment of God's purpose. Even with this knowledge, the knowledge alone does not make one capable; practice is necessary and practice takes perhaps a whole life. Every day one seems to make more mistakes. This is not really so, but one's sight becomes more keen.

What of those who do not think of all this? Every change of mood or emotion changes their actions, words and thoughts, and so they can never accomplish the things that they have come to accomplish. All their life is passed in failure and in mistakes, and in the end they gain what they have made. So it is always true that life is an opportunity, and every moment of life is valuable, to be able to handle oneself, and if one has done this, one has accomplished a great deal.

The key of the mind lies in God-realization.

30

THE MIND is made after the body. It is therefore that its form is that of the body. We read in the Old Testament that the heavens were made after the earth. The real place where the heavens are made is within man. The mind is made of all one learns, one experiences, one loves, and one remembers. It is therefore that man is that which his mind contains. If his mind contains a sorrow, man is sorrowful; if his mind contains joy, he is joyous; if it contains success, he is successful. If it contains failure, failure awaits him; everywhere he may move, he will find failure. The mind is an accommodation in which man collects all that he learns and experiences in life.

In short, man is his mind. How true, therefore, the claim of the dervishes is; sitting on the bare earth, clad in rags, they address one another: "O, King of Kings! O, Monarch of Monarchs!" That is their usual way of addressing one another. Their voice is the voice of true democracy, for this claim of theirs is the expression of their being conscious of the kingdom of God.

The mind is not only the treasure-house of all one learns, but, creative by nature, the mind improvises upon what it learns and creates not only in imagination, but it finishes its task when the imagination becomes materialized. The heavens or the infernal regions, all are the creations of the mind and all are experienced in the mind. But there is the question, "Is the body not born with a mind; did the mind not exist before the body?" Yes, it did exist as an *akasha*, an accommodation. And then the question, "How was this accommodation formed, on any certain model or design?"

The first design of that *akasha* is molded upon the impression that falls deeply upon the soul, the soul coming toward manifestation from the infinite Spirit. If we picture the infinite Spirit as the sun, the soul is as its ray. The nature of the soul is to gather on its way all that it can gather and it happens to gather, and make a mold out of it. It is this impression which has helped this first mold of the mind to be formed, to manifest its original nature and character through the body with which it is connected and identified.

The impression of the nature and character of the parents, of the ancestry, of the nation and the race, follows after the first impression that the soul has taken on its way. If it happens to be the impression of one personality falling upon the mind going towards manifestation, in the life of that person, the distinct character of a certain personality who lived in the past will show clearly. It is in this that the secret of the doctrine of reincarnation, which the Hindus have held, can be recognized.

There are souls who come from the infinite to the finite existence and there are spirits who return from the finite existence to the infinite. Their meeting-ground is on the way.

It may be one impression or it may be several impressions which help to mold this *akasha*, which after it is once connected with the body becomes the mind. For the mind cannot be complete before it has gained knowledge and experience by the help of the physical body.

The question, "Those who leave the body and pass away from the earth, is their mind not complete without the body?" may be answered that their mind is already completed by the experience they have had in their life on earth through the medium of the physical body.

* * *

Question: *What do you mean by the secret of reincarnation as a doctrine of the Hindus? It did not explain* karma.

Answer: *Karma* is another side of reincarnation. What I am saying is why some are born with a genius for art, music, painting, etc. Why are they born like this? The Hindus say it is the reincarnation of a great genius. The child does not only inherit from the nation, the parents, the races, etc., but also certain impressions are gained by the soul from some spirit as he passes through.

Question: *Is there some law when one comes on earth? It does not happen in a haphazard way?*

Answer: This very subtle problem is very difficult to explain. We are helped by understanding the meaning of accident and intention. They are two things, distinct, one intention and one accident. It helps us if we try to discover what is hidden behind accident. Then we come to the intention in the scheme of the working of the whole. Everything has a purpose, nothing is an accident. But there is accident to our mind, so accident exists for us like a shadow. Neither has a shadow real existence, nor accident. As the idea of accident goes on, it attracts accidents more and more, i.e. a person may wander for six months in Paris and he will not find a thief, but for a thief it will not take six hours to find one, for the law of attraction works. There is a verse in the Qur'an which explains this very well: "Not one atom moves without the command of God." Intention is behind every activity, and intention which we do not know we call accident.

Question: *Is the mind complete when it no longer has a body? Some people die very young.*

Answer: The mind is complete according to the experience it has. Then you can call it a mind. As long as the mind is not formed, the soul has not become individualized. It is not the body which becomes individualized, the mind becomes individualized through the mastery of the body. The mind as a record begins as soon as the child sees and hears. The body is like a machine that the soul takes and recalls every impression upon it.

Question: *Does the soul not come on earth then many times?*

Answer: It is very difficult to define "soul." The best answer is, the soul is the ray of the sun, which is the infinite Spirit.

The ray is an action of the sun; it is the ray itself. It manifests and returns as man inhales and exhales. Man's breath is himself; the existence is the one whose action it is. So is the soul we speak of.

Question: *Does the soul retain the experiences gained on earth?*

Answer: This brings one to the ultimate truth. You see, the light in all its forms is the light of the sun. In the gas, in the electric light, candle, star, planet, it is all a property of the sun, but we call it by different names. Soul is the life and light itself; it is God's own being. It manifests outwardly, and because of the smallness of the channels through which it comes, becomes small. But it is larger than we can possibly imagine. When the light is put out, it is not lost, for it is the property of the sun.

Every experience, even of animals, germs, are all collected and all remain in the one mind, which is the mind of God. It is distributed at the same time to different souls, and the closer we are, the more we benefit. And so we all have the right to make use of the storehouse of God. Therefore, spiritual people have been inspirational physicians, scientists, kings, judges, inventors, and statesmen because they get the key to this storehouse of knowledge. Scientists such as Edison may not appear to be spiritual, but their souls touched the storehouse of knowledge and they got inspiration. Solomon said, "There is nothing new under the sun."[31] All the knowledge that ever was is stored in the storehouse of God and can be gained in accordance to our openness.

31

THE MIND is not only the *akasha* which contains all one learns and experiences through life, but among the five different aspects of the mind, each having its own work, there is one aspect which especially may be called the mind, which shows the power of the Creator. All we see before our eyes, all the objects made by the skill of man, conditions brought about in life, favorable or unfavorable, they are all the creation of the human mind, of one mind or of many minds. Man's failures in life, together with the impression of limitation which man has, keep him ignorant of that great power which is hidden in the mind.

Man's life is the phenomenon of his mind. Man's happiness and success, man's sorrows and failures, are mostly brought about by his own mind, of which man knows so little. If this secret were known by all, no person in this world would be unhappy, no soul would have had failure. For unhappiness and failure both are unnatural. The natural is all man wants and wishes to have. No doubt, first one must know what one wants, and the next question is how to get it. The words of Emerson support this argument: "Beware of what you want, for you will get it."[32]

The whole life is one continual learning, and for the one who really learns from life, the knowledge is never enough. The more one learns the more there is to learn. The secret of this idea is in the Qur'an: "'Be,' God said, and then it became." The seers and knowers of life do not know this only in theory but it is their own life's experience.

There is a story told among the Hindus about a magic tree. A man was traveling in the hot sun towards the woods.

He became so tired that he felt like sitting under the shade of a tree. Then he thought, "If there were a little mattress to sit on, it would be better than stones," and as he looked he saw the mattress already there. Then he thought, "The tree is so hard to lean against," and when he turned, he saw there was a cushion already existing. Then he thought, "This mattress is too hard, if I had a cushion to sit on at the same time, now I am so tired" and it was there. Then he thought, "If I had some cooling syrup to drink, it would be very nice," and then he saw someone bringing him syrup. He was astonished and very glad. Then he thought, "This tree is not enough. It would be nice to have a house," and a beautiful little house was there. Then he thought, "Walking in the woods is very tiring, so I must have a chariot," and the chariot and the horses were there. He was very astonished and could not understand. Then he thought, "Is this all true or is it only imagination?" And then everything disappeared; only the hard stones remained and the tree above.

That is the story of the mind. The mind has the power to create—it creates everything. But out of what does it create? Out of the maze of *maya,* a substance subject to change, to death and destruction. However, the power of the mind is beyond question. And does this not teach us that mostly our unhappiness and our failures are caused more by our own minds than by the mind of another, and if caused by the mind of another then our mind is not in working order.

The knowledge of the power of the mind is then worth knowing when the moral conception of life is understood better: when man knows what is right and what is wrong, what is good and what is bad, and judges himself only, and sees these two opposite things in his own life, person and character. For man sees the folly of another and wishes to judge another when his sense of justice is not wide awake. Those whose personalities have brought comfort and healing to their fellowmen were the ones who only used the faculty of justice to judge themselves, who tried to correct themselves of their own follies, and being engaged in correcting themselves had hardly time in their life to judge another. The teaching of Christ: "Judge not, lest ye be judged,"[33] will always prove the greatest example to be followed.

The mind is a magic shell, a shell in which a design is made by the imagination, and the same imagination is materialized on the surface. The question, "Then why does not all we think come true; why is all we wish not always realized?" may be answered that by our limitedness we, so to speak, bury the divine creative power in our mind. Life confuses us so much that there is hardly among a thousand one person who really knows what he wants; and perhaps among a million there is one who knows why he wants it. And even among millions you will not find one with the knowledge of why he should want it and why he should not want it. With all the power of the mind one thing must be remembered: "Man proposes, God disposes" will always prove true when man's desire stands against the will of God almighty. Therefore, the path of the saints in life has been to seek with resignation the will of God, and in this way swim with the tide, so that with the accomplishment of their wish, the purpose of God may be fulfilled.

32

THE MIND has five different aspects. These are distinguished as the different departments of the mind, which have their own work to do. First, the heart, which feels and which contains the four other aspects of mind in itself. Second, the mind, which creates thought and imagination. Third, memory. Fourth, the will which holds the thought. And fifth is the ego, that conception of mind which claims: "I."

There is no mind without a body, for the body is a vehicle of the mind and is also made by the mind, not the same mind, but by other minds. The child does not only inherit the form and features of his parents and ancestors but their nature and character, in other words their mind, which molds its mind and body. The mind is not only the creator of thought, but a receptacle of all that falls upon it. The mind performs part of its work as ears, as eyes, as the mouth to taste, as the nostrils to smell, and as the skin to feel the touch. The awakened mind makes the body sensitive to all different feelings. The sleeping mind makes the body drowsy. At the same time the fineness of the body has its influence in making the mind finer, and the denseness of the body makes the mind dense. Therefore, the mind and body act and react upon one another.

When there is harmony between the mind and the body, health is secure and affairs will come right. It is the inharmony between mind and body which most often causes sickness and affairs go wrong. When the body goes south and the mind north, then the soul is pulled asunder, then there is no happiness. The secret of mysticism therefore, is to feel, think, speak and act at the same time, for then all that is said, or felt, or done, becomes perfect.

The different minds in the world may be likened to various mirrors, capable of projecting reflections and subject to reflect all that falls upon them. No one, however great in wisdom and power, can claim being free from influences. It is like the mirror claiming, "I don't reflect all that falls upon me." Only the difference between the wise and foolish is that the wise turns his back to what he must not reflect; the foolish one does not only reflect the undesirable thought, but most proudly owns it.

The mind is creative and the mind is destructive. It has both powers. No thought ever born of the mind, be it even for a second, is lost. Thought has its birth and death as a living being, and the life of the thought is incomparably longer than that of the living beings in the physical body. The relation of the thought which is created by a certain mind to that mind is that of the child to its parents. It is therefore that man is responsible not only for his action, but even for his thought. Souls would become frightened if they had a glimpse of the record of the thoughts they have created, without meaning to create them, under the spell of their ever changing moods. The Prophet has said that this life of the world, which has once been so attractive, will one day appear before them as a horrible witch; they will fly from it and will cry, "Peace, peace."

It would not be an exaggeration if one called the mind a world. It is the world that man makes in which he will make his life in the hereafter, as a spider weaves its web to live in. Once a person thinks of this problem, he begins to see the value of the spiritual path, the path in which the soul is trained not to be owned by the mind but to own it, not to become a slave of the mind, but to master it.

* * *

Question: *Which part of the mind makes the dream?*

Answer: The mind itself, that which creates thought and imagination. But there are three functions which go together in making the dream: the memory, the imagination, and the ego. In every dream there is the ego. The clearer the mind, the clearer the dream, and the subtler the mind, the subtler the dream. A dream is an instrument which tells man in what condition his mind is. Why has a dream its influence upon life? It is because the mind has its influence upon life.

Question: *What did you mean by saying, "The body is made by the mind, not the same mind, but by other minds?"*

Answer: This means the mind, before the body was made, was only an *akasha*. The experience that is gained through the body as a vehicle has become its knowledge, and it is knowledge which makes it mind. The *akasha*, which becomes the mind after the soul is born on earth, has already gathered some indistinct knowledge from various minds with which it came in contact while coming on earth, perhaps more from one mind than from others; in that case it has won more character of that one soul who passed from earth. Upon this, that *akasha* or mind has gained the knowledge or the mentality from the parents, from their ancestors, its race, and from the particular grade of evolution of that particular time of the whole humanity.

Question: *Can our illnesses be produced by the fault of others? Are we, for instance, always at fault when we fall ill?*

Answer: Man is always at fault, at a thousand faults. Illness can have several causes: inharmony between the mind and the body; inharmony in life. Illness is inharmony. If one will avoid inharmony, one will be well. This is the key to life. The first thing is to make peace with oneself, and that gives the strength of a thousand. If falling down by trying to do good to others, one has done no good to others, but if one were so strong that he could stand alone, that would be good work. The idea is this: we must first be concerned with ourselves, make our thought, word and action harmonious; then we give example to every one, and this must sooner or later have its effect.

If we only knew, there is no use troubling about others. We must try to correct ourselves, because there is no end to the correction we need in every thing. An awakened soul does not concern itself with the faults of others, but is concerned with itself and takes itself to task.

Question: *What is meant by feeling, thinking, speaking and acting at the same time?*

Answer: For instance in our prayers, in the elevation service; when we say a prayer we must realize its meaning, feel its effect, and perform the movements. It is feeling, speaking, thinking and acting at the same time. It means all our activities are devoted to one direction, and this concentration of every form into one action has the perfect power.

In the East, knowing this, they have a custom to make a certain food with a certain color for the sense of sight, also to give it a certain savor for the sense of taste, and also to give a fragrance. Thus, all the senses are given sustenance, fed at the same time as the body is fed; that may be called a perfect experience.

Question: *Is thought only killed or finished by another thought?*

Answer: Yes. A kind thought will kill a cruel thought. The thing is that man always remains like a child, something of childishness always remains. To be really grown up is the ripening, and when the mind is not ripening, it is raw, unripe, and that troubles a person because ripe fruit gives pleasure, happiness. And if the person does not become ripe, the purpose of life is not fulfilled.

Many people say, "I don't mind how I act in life, what people think." Then there is no fulfilment of life. The fulfilment of life's purpose is to mind, not to mind others but to mind ourselves. So if we knew what to mind, we would only mind ourselves.

Question: *Is the mind the world in which one will live in the hereafter?*

Answer: Yes.

Question: *Has life in the hereafter development, opportunity and help?*

Answer: Yes, for the mind is creative. It retains its creative tendency all through, here and in the hereafter. Since the mind is creative, it is progressive, and so there is opportunity of progressing here and in the hereafter.

33

BREATH[34] is the medium between the outer life and the inner life. By the help of breath, the elements necessary for the body can be attracted, and by the help of the breath thoughts and inspiration can be gained. By the help of breath, all that is undesirable in the body and mind can be expelled. The secret of telepathy, of reading the thought, has the science of breath as its mystery. When one wishes to draw inspiration from within, the breath is the key. Breath is a life current. Its value is known to so few. Breath in itself is a phenomenon. But the phenomenon becomes manifest when once the breath is fully mastered.

The law of transmutation is also the secret of breath. What we give and gain from another without seeing or hearing, which we only realize as a result of the contact with someone, that is the effect of breath. For by the medium of breath there is always something given and taken. So few are aware of it. In the presence of someone, one feels an inclination to laugh; in the presence of another, one has a desire to cry. The contact with one makes a person feel cheerful, with another sorrowful. Sometimes without there being one word spoken between two people, thoughts and feelings are transferred, without people knowing it, through the current of breath. Breath is a link with which one individual is connected with another individual, and space does not make a difference if once the connection of the breath is established. The communication will be sure and clear if only the wire is tied to sympathetic hearts.

There is much in common with the science of electricity and the science of breath. The day is not very far off when science and mysticism both will meet on the same ground in the realization of the electricity which is hidden in the breath.

* * *

Question: *If through breath one can come in contact with another being, can one also come in contact with the dead?*

Answer: Yes.

Question: *Which is the most important part of breath, the inhalation or the exhalation?*

Answer: Both.

Question: *What is the link between the breath and the will?*[35]

Answer: The will is as the rider and the breath the rein in his hand.

Question: *If breath is the vehicle of will, in what way is the will the link between men?*

Answer: As one has to live in the midst of the world, so one has no other place to breathe between sky and earth. In this way one cannot, however much one wishes, fully escape being connected with others. This is why I have often said that we are interdependent upon one another. One cannot get out of the situation. The action of speaking, hearing, seeing, and being seen, they all have their medium of breath. No sooner has the breath ceased to hold the organs of the body in perfect condition than that man is no longer living.

Question: *What is the role of the will in the interdependence of man?*

Answer: The will plays a most important part. By the power of will we master life, if only wisdom is at our side. If not, the same will may become injurious and harmful to us.

Question: *In healing, is not most of the work done by breath?*

Answer: Yes.

Question: *Is intellectual knowledge located in the brain and wisdom located in the heart?*

Answer: Neither of these are located in brain or heart, only intellectual knowledge has much to do with the brain and wisdom comes from within the heart. But in wisdom, the heart and head both work.

Wisdom is spiritual knowledge. The best explanation of wisdom is perfect knowledge; that is, the knowledge of life within and without.

What is gained by intuition, the mind makes it clear, and yet often it is the mind which spoils the intuition, for the mind interferes with the intuition. If the mind did not stand as a hindrance to intuition, every person would be intuitive, for intuition is more natural and more easy than the reasoning of the mind. The intuition by nature is clear; the characteristic of the mind is confusion. If the intuition is disturbed, it is because it has been confused by the mind. However, it is not necessary to give up reason for intuition. But naturally cultivate the faculty of intuition without letting it stand in the way of reason.

For instance, if a person always did everything trusting to his intuition, he would have many difficulties, for very often the intuition will be wrong, for the reason that as a child he did not begin with intuition. So often reason, disguised as intuition, deceives him. While developing the faculty of intuition, if we did not mind being deceived, and risked, then in time the mind would not play its tricks, and the intuition will be powerful enough to manifest clearly. In time a person of finer feelings will be able to perceive the voice of intuition and will learn to discriminate between intuition and reason.

One thing must be remembered and that is to perceive the first suggestion that rises in the heart before it is disturbed by the action of the mind. If that opportunity is lost, it will not take one moment for the reason to attack the intuition and establish its own place there. What comes from without is not intuition; intuition is something which rises from our own heart and brings satisfaction, ease and happiness.

Question: *Do all experiences reach the brain through the nerve centers?*

Answer: Yes, mostly conveyed by the breath, but in this I do not mean the breath we inhale through the nostrils. Through the pores of the skin we breathe also, though the main stream of breath is that which we inhale through the nostrils and which is termed *prana* in Vedantic terms.

34

İT HAS BEEN ASKED of the sages and the thinkers of all times by the seekers after truth to explain the meaning of the word soul. Some have tried to explain and some have given an answer which may be difficult for everyone to understand. In the meaning of the word soul many thinkers differ, although all mystics arrive at the same understanding of the idea of soul.

As the air, by being caught in the water, becomes a bubble for the moment, and as a wave of the air being caught in a hollow vessel becomes a sound, so intelligence caught by the mind and body becomes the soul. Therefore, intelligence and soul are not two things; it is only a condition of intelligence which is the soul. Intelligence in its original aspect is the essence of life, the spirit of God. But when this intelligence is caught in an accommodation such as body and mind, its predisposition of knowing—its original nature—then knows, and that knowing soul becomes consciousness.

The difference between consciousness and the soul is that the soul is like a mirror, and consciousness is a mirror which shows a reflection in it. The Persian word *ruh* and the Sanskrit word *atma* mean the same, that is soul. There is another word in the English language which means one or single: sole. Although different in spelling, yet it is expressive of the same idea, that the soul is that part of our being in which we realize our being to be one single being. When one thinks of the body it has many organs. When one thinks of the mind it has various thoughts. When one thinks of the heart it has many feelings. But when one thinks of the soul in the right sense of the word, it is one single being. It is above division and therefore it is the soul which really can be called an individual. Very often the philosophers have used this name for the body, mind and consciousness, all three.

Sufism originally comes from the word *safa*, which means purity. This purity is attained by purifying the soul from all the foreign attributes that it has acquired, thereby discovering the real nature and character of the soul. Pure water means something which is in its original element, with no sugar or milk mixed with it. If it happens that there is sugar and milk in the water, then the one who wishes to analyze it must separate them and will try to see water in its pure condition.

Sufism, therefore, is the analyzing of the self, the self which has for the moment become a mixture of three things, of body, mind and soul. By separating the two outer garments of the soul, the Sufi discovers the real nature and character of the soul, and in this discovery lies the secret of the whole life. Rumi has said in the *Mathnawi*[36] that life on the earth is a captivity of the soul. When one looks at the air being caught by the water, one sees the meaning of Rumi, that something which is free to move about becomes captive by the atoms of water for a time and loses its freedom for that moment.

Man, in all conditions of life, whatever be his rank, position or possession, has troubles, pains, difficulties. Where do these come from? From his limitation. But if limitation were natural, why should he not be contented with his troubles? Because it is not natural to the soul. The soul, who is by nature free, feels uncomfortable in the life of limitations in spite of all that this world can offer. When the soul experiences the highest degree of pain, it refuses all that this world can offer in order to fly from the spheres of the earth and seek the spheres of liberty, the freedom of which was the soul's previous possession.

There is a longing hidden beneath all other longings man has, and that longing is for freedom. This longing is sometimes satisfied by a walk in solitude, in the woods, when one is left alone to be by oneself for a time, when one is fast asleep and even dreams do not trouble one, and when one is in meditation in which for the moment the activities of body and mind both are suspended. Therefore, the sages have preferred solitude and have always shown love for nature. And they have adopted meditation as the method of attaining that goal which is the freedom of the soul.

* * *

Question: *Is the name Adam associated with breath?*

Answer: In Dutch the word *adem* and in German the word *atem* means breath. I think this word comes from the same origin as *atma*. But in the Persian language *dum* means breath and *adam* means when the breath begins to move, when the life begins to move.

Question: *Does this mean there is a relation between breath and soul? Will you explain the relation?*

Answer: Someone asked the Prophet the meaning of the soul, and the Prophet said, "a ray, an activity of breath." If I were to give an interpretation of this, I would say, "an action of life, a movement of life." When life moved, it turned into breath. But if I were to say in my own words what this creation is, I would say, "It is the breath of God." And if one asked, "What is the end of it?" I would only say, "The indrawing breath." Nothing is lost. It is only inhaling and exhaling. The creation and what is called annihilation, in the end it is only the breath of God.

Question: *How does the Sufi separate the two outer garments of the soul?*

Answer: I have explained this through all my teaching, from the beginning to the end, in practices, concentrations, meditations; this is the only explanation that I give because that is the object which the soul has to realize in the end, and our every effort in the spiritual path is towards God-realization.

Question: *If you believe in the Sufi point of view of reincarnation, how do you explain that feeling we sometimes have upon meeting a person for the first time, of having known that person before? In the same way, one sometimes has the feeling of having seen a certain landscape or place before.*

Answer: The Sufi point of view of reincarnation has been fully explained in a book called *The Phenomenon of the Soul*.[37] Yet one cannot explain this idea, which is an abstract idea and which has many complexities, more briefly. Although the soul that comes on earth does not only inherit the qualities of the parents and ancestors, it also brings with it a knowledge that it has gained on its way. But this can be more understood by reading the ten lectures given this summer on the subject of metaphysics.[38]

35

THE INTELLIGENCE becomes captive to knowledge. That which is its sustenance limits it, reduces it, and all the pain and pleasure, birth and death is experienced by the intelligence in this captivity which we call life. Death, in point of fact, does not belong to the soul, and so it does not belong to the person. Death comes to what the person knows, not to the person. Life lives, death dies. But the mind which has not probed the depth of the secret of life becomes perplexed and unhappy over the idea of death. A person once went to a Sufi and asked him, "What happens after death?" He said, "Ask this question of someone who is to die, of some mortal being, which I am not."

Intelligence is not only a knowing faculty but is creative at the same time. The whole manifestation is the creation of the intelligence. Time and space both are nothing but the knowledge of the intelligence. The intelligence, confined to this knowledge, becomes limited, but when it becomes free from all knowledge, then it experiences its own essence, its own being. It is this which the Sufis call the process of unlearning, which purifies or makes intelligence free from knowledge. It is the glimpses of that experience which is called ecstasy, for then the intelligence has an independent joy which is true happiness. The soul is happiness in itself; nothing else can make the soul fully happy but self-realization. The phenomenon which the intelligence creates by its creative power becomes a source of its own delusion, and as the spider becomes caught in its own web, so the soul becomes imprisoned in all it has created. This picture we see in the lives of individuals and of the multitude.

Motive gives power and at the same time it is motive

which limits power. For the power of the soul is greater than any motive. But it is the consciousness of the motive which stimulates the power and yet robs the soul of its power.

The Hindus have called the whole phenomenon of life by the name *maya*, which means a puzzle, and once the true nature and character of this puzzle is realized, the meaning of every word of language becomes untrue, except the one Truth which words cannot explain. Therefore, the soul may be considered to be a condition of God, a condition which makes the Only Being limited for a time; and the experience gained in this time with its ever-changing joy and pain is interesting, and the fuller the experience, the wider becomes the vision of life. And what one has to experience in life is its true being. The life which everyone knows is this momentary period of the soul's captivity. Beyond this one knows nothing. Therefore, every seeming change that takes place, one calls it death or decay. Once the soul has risen above this illusive phase of life by climbing on the top of all that is besides the soul itself, it experiences in the end that happiness for which this whole creation took place. The discovering of the soul is the uncovering of God.

The word intelligence as it is known by us, or spoken in everyday language, does not give a full idea. Especially the word intelligence, used by modern science, will only convey to us something which is the outcome of matter or energy. But according to the mystic, intelligence is the primal element, or the cause as well as the effect. While science acknowledges it as the effect, the mystic sees in this the cause.

One will question how intelligence can create this dense earth, which is matter; there must be energy behind it. But this question comes because we separate intelligence from energy or matter. In point of fact, it is the spirit which is matter, and matter which is spirit. The denseness of the spirit is matter and the fineness of matter is spirit. Intelligence becomes intelligible by turning into denseness; that denseness, being manifest to its own view, creates two objects: the self and what is known by the self. And there comes of necessity a third object, the medium with which the person knows what he knows, such as the sight or the mind. And it is these three aspects of life which are at the root of the idea of the Trinity.[39] The moment these three are realized as one, life's purpose is fulfilled.

As matter evolves, so it shows intelligence. And when one studies the growing evolution of the material world, one will find that at each step of evolution the material world has shown itself to be more intelligent, which is finished in the evolution of the human race. But this outcome of the development of matter is only the predisposition of what we call matter which is manifested in the end. And everything in nature is the evidence of this truth, even in the vegetable world, when we see that it is the seed which is the root. And therefore, it is intelligence which comes as the very effect, as the cause.

* * *

Question: *Does motive limit the intensity of power?*

Answer: Certainly. Motive is a shadow upon the intelligence. It might seem that it increases the power, but no doubt at the end one finds out that it robs the power, although the higher the motive, the higher is the soul. The greater is the motive, the greater the person. When the motive is beneath one's ideal, then it is the fall of man, and when the motive is his ideal, it is his rise. According to the width of motive, man's vision is wide and according to the power of the motive, man's strength is great.

THE SOUL'S JOURNEY

TOWARDS MANIFESTATION

THE MANIFESTED SOUL

TOWARDS THE GOAL

THE SOUL
TOWARDS THE GOAL

36

THE SOUL, during its journey towards manifestation and during its stay on any plane, whether in the sphere of the angels, of the *jinns* or of human beings, feels attraction towards its source and goal. Some souls feel more attraction than others, but there is an unconscious or conscious indrawing felt by every soul. It is the ignorant soul, ignorant of its source and goal, who dreads leaving the spheres it has become attached to; it is the soul who knows not what is beyond who is afraid to be lifted up above the ground its feet are touching. Is the fish afraid of going to the depth of the sea? Fish apart, there even are men who are born on earth, who have been brought up on the earth, but who make a practice of diving deep into the sea and bringing out from there pearl shells. There are seamen who are happier on the sea than on the land. And their heroism, to those unaccustomed to the phenomenon of water, gives a great bewilderment.

Life is interesting in its every phase; on the journey towards manifestation, as well as on the soul's return towards the goal. Every moment of life has its peculiar experience, one better than the other, one more valuable than the other. In short, life may be said to be full of interest. Sorrow is interesting as well as joy. There is a beauty in every phase of life, if only one can learn to appreciate it.

What dies? It is death that dies, not life. What is the soul then? The soul is life; it never touches death. Death is its illusion, its impression. Death comes to something which it holds, not to itself. The soul becomes accustomed to identifying itself with the body that adorns it, with the environment that surrounds it, with the names by which it is known, by its rank and possessions, which are only outward signs which belong to the world of illusion. The soul, absorbed in its childlike fancies, in the things that it values and gives importance to, and in the beings that it attaches itself to, blinds itself by the veils of enthusiasm over it, thus covering its own truth with a thousand veils over its own eyes.

What is the return journey? Where does one return? When does one return? The return begins from the time the flower has come to a full bloom; from the moment the plant has touched its summit, from the time the object, the purpose for which a soul is born on earth, is fulfilled. For then there is nothing to hold it, and the soul naturally draws back like breath drawn in. But is man dead by drawing in his breath? So the soul is not dead by its drawing in, though apparently it gives the man dying and those who notice it an impression of death.

The physical body may be likened to a clock. It has its mechanism and it requires winding, and this winding keeps it up. And it is the healthiness of the physical body which is able by its magnetic power to hold the soul which functions in it. As this body for some reason or other, either because of a disorder or by having been worn out, loses that power of keeping together by which it holds the soul in it, this function gives way and the soul naturally departs, leaving the material body as one would throw away a coat that one no longer needs.

The connection of the body and the soul is like man's attachment to his dress. It is man's duty to keep his dress in good order, for he needs it to live in the world, but it is ignorance, a great ignorance indeed, when man forgets himself and knows himself as his dress. And so man does as a rule. How few in this world stop to think on this subject: whether it is myself, this body, or whether myself is apart from this body, higher or greater than this body, more precious and long-living than this body? What then is mortality? There is no such thing as mortality except the illusion and the impression of that illusion which man keeps before himself as a fear during his lifetime and as an impression after he has passed from this earth. Nevertheless, as it says in the Qur'an, "All souls have come from God and to him is their return."[40]

* * *

Question: *Would it be possible for a soul to come on earth, and yet remain free from illusion and attachment?*

Answer: Yes, but to some extent there must be illusion and attachment. But it can be even the least attachment and illusion. But if there were not illusion and attachment, it would be just like day all the time, and no night. We need day and night both. We can enjoy the sun by having had the night; the rising and the setting of the sun, both give us joy, happiness. But in the illusion and the attachment there is a motive power, and by that a purpose in life is accomplished. And if there were not attachment and illusion, even to a small extent, the soul would not be able to hold the body, because even that is attachment. Therefore, another thing in connection with this is that there are many people who become very ill and yet they do not die. For years and years they go through an illness, and they do not die. The reason is the attachment to the body. They may say they would like to leave the body, but still they are attached to it. And as long as they hold this attachment, the soul cannot leave it. Because attachment is a soul power, the magnetism is there.

Question: *Are there not three different kinds of space? Will you explain a little more on this question?*[41]

Answer: If you say that there are four dimensions, I will say that there are four. If you say that there are three, I will say that there are three, because there are two ways of looking at it. The three kinds of space are this sphere, and the sphere of the *jinn*, and the sphere of the angels. And then there is the other aspect or way of looking at it according to the explanation of the four dimensions: the length, the breadth, and the height, and besides that there is the fourth dimension—that is what the mystic calls the space within.

There came a scientist one day to hear my lecture. He was very interested in some of the ideas, but he asked me: "If you can say 'in the body' then I can understand, but when you say 'within,' now I cannot understand what you mean by this." He was right. But I explained to him what the space is. Space is that which accommodates; that is the definition of space. Then your mind is a space also; it accommodates a space which is wider than the world. Your eye is a space also. But the mind is not necessarily the brain; nor are these eyes, which outwardly appear to be the eyes, the only space, but behind it there is another space connected with the eye. Therefore, the eye is a rope between man and God. Therefore, it is "I." It means the self; it has a different spelling, but it is the same thing: the ego. It sees. What sees? God himself sees through it. Therefore, there is a direct road between the earth and heaven through the eyes. The eyes which appear before us are two. The sight is one. That is the third eye. The third eye is where the two eyes are linked together and become one. That is the key to the whole Egyptian mystery where there is the sign of the eye. In that eye there is eye and ego both.

And when we say that there are three different kinds of space, naturally there are three different kinds of time, which are incomparable. Time in the higher heavens is more durable, is longer compared with the time of this world. Time in the highest heaven is still longer. And therefore there are three different worlds, and three different times. However, to the one who realizes the ultimate truth, time and space both are of little importance. He rises above it. This yard and foot and inch are nothing. Once you begin to think of eternity, a day or month or year is nothing.

Question: *A rapid run seems to give a less profound experience than the slow progress. Is it one's choice, or a question of temperament?*

Answer: I should say it is a question of temperament. But I think that the happy medium is the best. Too slow is monotonous, and too quick is undesirable. I think the joy of the journey is in the balance. For instance, if by the speed of the ant or worm or germ, if by that speed man traveled, he would not go very far; he is not made to travel like that. He is made to travel in his own way, at his own speed. But when he adopts an artificial speed, that is not his own speed. Therefore, always remember, a person who will go in the airplane or railway train, he will not enjoy the full pleasure of the journey as the man who goes traveling on foot. I one day met a gentleman in the train. He said, "I had been on this journey about twenty times, and then traveled it walking." That is the joy. The man who travels in the train, he cannot imagine to what extent the one who walks can enjoy, because that is his natural speed. In everything we can see the same thing. From the gramophone we hear the human voice, but it loses the magnetism, because it is the human voice which gives the full joy to a human being.

Question: *Do those who die with an object unaccomplished do so in a moment of despair?*

Answer: It so happens that when their mind is not strong enough to hold that object which they want to accomplish, then it gives way. Besides that, sometimes the body is not in a fit state to hold it, and therefore one dies with the object unaccomplished. But that is in accordance to one's mind, not in the scheme of nature. It would be in harmony with the scheme of nature if one's object were accomplished as well, because that is the natural death.

Question: *Do those who commit suicide out of despair also do so out of illusion?*

Answer: Yes, certainly. It is just like breaking two things which are attached to one another. It is cutting by will, separating by will, things which are not meant to be separated. The scheme of nature would have accomplished something. By separating them, they have deprived themselves of what the scheme of nature would have given them.

37

LIFE AND DEATH are both contrary aspects of one thing, and that is change. If there remains anything of death with the soul who has passed away from this earth, it is the impression of death according to the idea it has of death. If the soul had a horror of death, it carries that horror with it. If it had an agitation against death, it carries that impression. Besides, the dying soul carries with itself the impression of the idea and regard that those surrounding it in life had for death, especially at the time of its passing from the earth. This change for some time paralyzes every activity of the soul. The soul which has become impressed by the idea that it held itself of death, and by the impression which was created by its surroundings round the death bed, is kept in a state of inertia, call it fear, horror, depression or disappointment.

It takes some time for the soul to recover from this feeling of inactivity. It is this which, from the metaphysical point of view, may be called purgatory. Once the soul has recovered from this state, it again begins to progress, advancing towards its goal on the tracks which it had laid before.

The picture of this idea may be explained thus: A simple man was told in jest by his friend that when a person is yawning, that is the sign of death. He was impressed by this idea and after once he had the experience of yawning, he thought certainly he was dead. He was very sad over his death and went to look for a grave for himself, despairing over the idea of how false friends are that no one came to his funeral. He found a hole in the ground dug by the wolves, and he thought to himself, "How nice, I do not need

to dig a grave for myself, at least that much is done for me."
He threw himself into that hole and was lying comfortably,
sorrowing over his death.

A man happened to pass that way who was looking for
someone to carry some of his load and who was talking to
himself, "If only I had someone in these woods who could
carry half of my load, it would be so nice." In answer to his
thought, he heard someone say, "Alas, now I am dead; if I
were living, I would certainly have helped you." This man
could not understand how a person who is dead would
speak. As he turned back and looked, he found a man lazily
lying in a hole dug in the ground. He thought that perhaps
he was ill; he could help him. He came near and asked,
"What is the matter with you?" The simpleton said, "Nothing
is the matter with me, I am quite well, only I am dead." The
man said, "How can you be dead? You do not look like a
dead man, you are speaking. How could you be dead and
speak at the same time? You are not dead." But the simpleton was good at argument; he still continued saying, "No,
no, I am dead!" until the man had to kick him out of that
hole. Then he got up and tried to believe that he was not
yet dead.

Behind this humorous story there is a wonderful secret
hidden. How many souls prove simple in believing the idea
of death and carrying with them the same idea while passing
from the earth to a life which is a greater life still. And how
many souls will we find in the world who believe the end
of life to be death, a belief in mortality which cannot be
rooted out from their minds. The whole teaching of Jesus
Christ has as its central theme to rise towards the realization
of immortality.

* * *

Question: *How can we make people believe in this immortality, and make them rise above the fear of death?*

Answer: Gradually, and not suddenly. Because suddenly,
the knowledge of truth frightens a person more than death.

It is therefore that the knowledge of truth is made a mysticism, a secret science. If not, there would be no necessity of hiding truth from one's fellow man, before whom one can bring anything, however precious, if it is for his good. And such spiritual wealth, the more you give, the more it is increased. By giving to another soul you have not lost, only gained. What one has is doubled when one has given to another. But the thing is that one must know whether a person is prepared. Do you know what happens sometimes when a person is fast asleep and you suddenly wake him? He gets a shock to his mind and body both, from which with great difficulty he recovers, and which does him a great deal of harm, physically and mentally. And it is the same thing with the truth. That is why all these initiations, all is secret; there is the vow of secrecy. If not, it would be no one's loss in giving the truth to any soul, to friend or foe, both. A sage would be as willing to give the truth to friend and foe. Because once he has raised the truth, there will be no longer a foe. The difficulty is that it cannot be given at once. One cannot place dinner before the newborn infant who must be fed first with milk.

Question: *Do some souls remain under the impression of death for a great length of time?*

Answer: Time in the next world is quite different from time here. Certainly, the length of the time which they have to pass through purgatory depends on how deep was the impression. The deeper the impression—the impression of the horror of death—the longer the time. The sages, the prophets, have shown their spiritual advancement at the moment of their death. That is the time when the truth comes out, and falseness has no chance to make a play. It is the last moment when the soul is passing from this earth. It then shows where is its heart, on the earth or in heaven. If it is on the earth, then the last time shows it. If it is in heaven, then also the last time shows it. Besides that, the person who has earned peace throughout his life, then he shows his wealth when passing away. That he is passing away peacefully, that shows his riches; and his willingness to meet with what comes in the life beyond, that shows his nobility.

Question: *Will you please tell us about the scenery of the* jinn *world; does that world interpenetrate this world?*

Answer: The scenery of the *jinn* world is peculiar to itself. It is the negative state of what one sees as positive in this world, but in more beauty than what one sees on the earth. In this way it interpenetrates. But at the same time it has its own peculiarity, which is incomparable with the beauty of this earth. The reason is that the manifestation on this plane has more limitations, owing to its rigidity. The higher the world, the less are the limitations to be met with.

Question: *You spoke in* The Mysticism of Sound[42] *of the power there is in the word. Would it not be of great influence if those who believe in a continuation of life in another world left off using the word "death," but spoke instead of that "passing over" or "passing into the unseen"?*

Answer: Much better.

Question: *Is there not much symbolism in the mirror, which is made to reflect objects by the substance called mercury, which was also an ancient name of the messenger of God?*

Answer: Yes, there is a great connection there. But the story of Hatim[43] also explains the same thing: that the princess was God, and the pearl that the princess wanted was the knowledge of God. And there was a lover of God, but he would not go and take that trouble which one has to take to obtain it. There was someone else ready: his work was to take the trouble and go deep, even if it was not for himself but for the others, and to get the knowledge and to give it to the one who has the love to have it. This also is the same thing.

Question: *Will you please speak about the subject of God's justice?*

Answer: By giving a little simile, I will show you what difference there is between man's justice and God's justice. There are children of the same father and they are quarreling over their toys. They're quarreling over toys, for which they have a reason. The one thinks that a certain toy is more attractive to him—why should he not possess it? The other says that toy was given to him, he must have it. Both have their reasons and both are just. But the father's justice is different from theirs. The father has not only given them the toys to play with, but at the same time he knows what the character of each child is, and what he wishes to bring out in that child, and whether that particular toy will help to bring out in him that which he wishes to come out. It happens, perhaps, that the toy seems poor to the child, and with his sense of justice he cannot understand why that toy was given to him and not to the other. If he were a grown-up child he would have accused his father of injustice. But one does not know the justice of one's father. One has to grow to that state of evolution where one's father is in order to understand the meaning behind it.

It is the same with the justice of God and man. Man's justice is covered by his limited experience in life, by his favor and disfavor, by his preconceived ideas, by the learning he has, which is nothing compared with the knowledge of God. When one compares the father with his innocent child, they are too near to be compared with God and man, where there is such a distance. If we counted the human beings that exist, they would be like drops compared with the ocean. There is no comparison between God and man. Therefore, man's justice is imperfect, God's justice is perfect.

And if one ever gets a glimpse of divine justice, the only way is first to believe in the justice of God, against all the proofs which contradict his justice. And there are many proofs which will contradict his justice. If one began to look at why this person is rich, why the other person is poor, why that person is in a high position, why this person has suffered so much, why the other has lived long and had a pleasant life—if one will judge their actions, their intelligence, their stage of evolution, one will not find justification. By judging thus, one will come to a conclusion when one will say, "Oh, there is no justice. It is all, perhaps, mechanical working behind it."

The idea of *karma* and reincarnation will satisfy one. But at the same time it will root out God behind it. Then God has no power, if everyone has the power of making his own *karma*. Root out God, then everything is mechanically working. If so, then there cannot be a machine without an engineer; for a machine there must be an engineer. If there is an engineer, then he must be powerful. Is he subject to his power, or the controller? If he is subject, then he is not powerful enough, then he is limited. Then he no more can be God. God is he who is perfect in his justice, in his wisdom, and in his power.

But if we question the cause of all such happenings which do not give us a justification, we then come to another question. And that is, "Can a composer give a certain justification to every note that he has given in his composition?" He can only say that, "It is the stream that has come out of my heart. I have tried to maintain certain laws, but if you ask me the justification of every note, I am unable to do it. I am not concerned with every note; I am concerned with the effect that the whole produces."

It is not true that there is no law. There is a law. But is law predominant or love? Law is a habit, and love is the being. Law is made, love was never made. It was, it is, and it will be. Therefore, love—what do we read in the Bible? God is love. So God is beyond the law. Love is above the law. Therefore, if we come to any solution to our ever rising question, "Why is it so?", it is not by the study of the law. Never. Increasing the study of the law will only give an increasing appetite and will never bring satisfaction. In diving deep into love, and letting the love inspire the law, that will open up a realm of seeing the law. Then we will see that there is nothing in this world which has no justification. It is inexplicable, but it is perceptible, that all has its justification. Then we shall not have one word to say that this is unjust. Even the cruelest thing we have seen. That is the point that the wise reach and call it the culmination of wisdom.

38

WHAT IS purgatory? Purgatory in Sufi terms may be called *kemal*, suspension of activity. If there is any death, it is still-ness or inactivity. It is just like a clock, which for some time has stopped, which wants another winding; and a little movement sets the clock going. So there comes the impulse of life, which, breaking through this cloud of mortality, makes the soul see the daylight after the darkness of the night. And what does the soul see in this bright daylight? It sees itself living as before, having the same name and form and yet progressing. The soul finds a greater freedom in this sphere and less limitation than it had previously experienced in its life on the earth.

Before the soul now is a world, a world not strange to it, but the world which it has made during its life on the earth. That which the soul has known as mind, that very mind to the soul now is a world. That which the soul called, while on earth, imagination is now before it a reality. If this world is artistic, it is the art produced by this soul. If there is the absence of beauty, that is also the neglect of the soul towards beauty while on earth.

The pictures of paradise, the ideas about the heavens, and the conception of the infernal regions now, to the soul, is an experience. Is the soul sent to one or the other place among the many who are rejoicing there or suffering for their sins? No. This is the kingdom that the soul has made while on earth, as a bird builds its nest to stay there during the autumn. This is the autumn of the soul, which is the hereafter. It passes this autumn in the world which it has made either agreeable or disagreeable for itself.

But one might ask, "Do you mean to say that the soul lives a solitary life in this world it has made?" No, how can it be solitary? This mind, the secret of which so few know in the world, this mind can be as large as the world and larger still. This mind can contain all that exists in the world and even all that the universe contains in itself. "But what a wonderful phenomenon," one might say. "I never thought that the mind could be so large; I thought the mind was even smaller than my body, that it was hidden somewhere in the corner of my brain." The understanding of mind indeed widens one's outlook on life. It first produces bewilderment and then the vision of the nature of God, which is a phenomenon in itself. Does one then see all those one has known while on the earth? Yes, especially those whom one has loved most and hated most.

What will be the atmosphere of this world? It will be the re-echo of the same atmosphere which one has created in the world. If one has learned while on earth how to create joy and happiness for oneself and for others, in the other world that joy and happiness will surround one. And if one has sown the seeds of poison while on earth, the fruits one has to reap there, one must reap there. That is where one sees justice as the nature of life. The idea of the prophets which one reads in the ancient scriptures, that there will be a Judgement Day and man will be called before the great Judge to answer for his deeds, must not be understood literally as it is said. In the first place the Judge would not have sufficient time to hear the numberless cases; since every soul would have a world full of faults, his merits would amount to nothing when compared with his faults. No, Judgement Day is every day and one knows it the more keen his sight becomes. Every hour, every moment in life has its judgement. As the Prophet has said, "The soul will have to give account for every grain of corn it eats." There is no doubt about it, but why especially the Judgement Day has been mentioned in the scriptures to take place in the hereafter is because in the hereafter one cover from the soul has been lifted up. Therefore, the judgement which every soul experiences here on earth and yet remains ignorant of, being unconscious of it, becomes more clearly manifest to the view of a soul who has passed from this earth.

What connection has the soul who has passed from the earth with those who are still on the earth? No doubt there is a wall now which divides those on this earth from those on the other plane, yet the connection of the heart still remains intact and unbroken as long as the link of sympathy is there. But why do the lovers of those who have passed away from the earth not know of the conditions of their beloveds on the other side? They know it in their souls, but the veils of the outer illusions of the physical world cover their heart. Therefore, they cannot get clear reflections through. Besides, it is not only the link of love and sympathy, but it is the belief in the hereafter, to the extent of conviction in that belief, which lifts those on earth to know about their beloved ones who have passed on to the other side. Those who deny the hereafter, they deny themselves that knowledge which is the essence of all learning. It is easier for those who have passed from the earth to the other side to get in touch with those on the earth, for they have one veil less than those on the earth.

* * *

Question: *Are the souls who have passed nearer to us than those who live with us?*

Answer: In one way they are nearer, and in another way they are further. They are nearer in this way: that if we wanted to get in connection with them, or they with us, it is more quickly and easily done than with the souls who are here on the earth. But in another way they are much further. When one sees the difference between the plane that we live on, and they, those on earth are nearer to us because we live on the same plane; therefore, there are many different means of communication.

Question: *Is it natural for the souls who have passed to come in contact with the souls on earth?*

Answer: Yes, it is quite natural.

Question: *How do these souls you are telling about move from place to place?*

Answer: They move from place to place much quicker, even beyond what one can imagine being on the earth. Their form is not so dense as the earthly form, yet they have a form. They are more capable of moving about than a bird. And it is for this reason that every child longs to have wings, because his soul feels deprived of that freedom which it has known. Therefore, the only consolation for a poor child is to think of fairies, that there are beings who move about with wings. It is therefore that one often dreams of flying.

Question: *What are they engaged in doing?*

Answer: They are engaged in the same thing, in what they have been doing before. Everything they have had here, they have there, but with a greater freedom. Because here they cannot improve upon it, hindered by the limitations of the earthly law. There they can improve it if there is only the impulse behind it towards improvement.

Question: *They do everything with the mind, not with the head?*

Answer: Yes.

Question: *Is the world of mind more beautiful than nature on earth?*

Answer: Certainly it is. For mind is nature also. Mind is an improvement upon nature, and natural at the same time. For instance, the idea of paradise is an improvement upon nature. And as now on earth, paradise is a mere imagination, but in the hereafter the same idea will become a reality.

Question: *Those who have made mental pictures of hell fire, will they literally experience that hell?*

Answer: Certainly. Omar Khayyam says, "Heaven is the vision of fulfilled desire, hell is the shadow of the soul on fire." Therefore, it is no use impressing people on the earth to experience horrors and tortures, except that they [these horrors?] offend us so much that we do not listen.

Question: *Does the soul in the hereafter live on old or new impressions?*

Answer: It is a continuation of the impressions of all that it has collected. If one knows how to throw them off, one need not take them with one. Then comes the question of mysticism. That is why, always, the wise have said to have constructive thoughts, the tendency to joy, beauty and happiness for ourselves and others, so that it will multiply and become more and more abundant, and in the hereafter this will make a world of happiness if one continues to keep that idea through life. It is the whole religion and philosophy there.

39

WHAT DOES a soul do after having arrived at the sphere of the *jinn*? It continues to do the same which it has been doing, right or wrong, good or bad. It goes along the same lines that it has gone through life. Is there no progress for that soul? Yes, there is, but in the same direction. No ultimate change necessarily takes place. Yes, the soul finds itself in more clear spheres and therefore knows its way better than it had known before when on earth.

What is its destination? The same destination may be hidden under a thousand objects; every soul is bound for the same goal. How can it be otherwise? Fancy how one becomes attached to a place where one has been before, how one is attracted to a spot in the solitude where once one sat and enjoyed the beauty of nature. How much then the soul must be attracted, either consciously or unconsciously, to its source, which is its eternal abode.

What connection do the souls who have passed from the earth have with others who have left the earth? No particular connection, except the connection which is made by the link of sympathy.

Do they all know of the conditions on the earth? Yes, if they care to. How can they know if they care to? Is there no wall between the people on the earth and those who have passed away from this earth? Yes, there is a wall, which only stands before those who are still on the earth, but not before the ones who have passed on to the other side. They rise above this wall, so they see, if they care to see, the condition of the world as clearly as we do, and even more so. Do they have to have some medium in order to observe the conditions on the earth, or can they observe without any medium? No, they must have a medium, a medium on the earth as their instrument. For they must have the physical eyes to see, and the physical ears to hear, and physical senses to experience life in the physical world.

Then what do they do in order to experience life in the physical world? They seek for an accommodation in the heart of a being on the earth and focus themselves on the mind of the person and receive through this medium all the knowledge and experience of this earth as clearly as this person himself. For instance, if a scientist wishes to learn something from the earth and he happens to focus himself upon the mind of an artist, an artist who knows nothing about science, and who will perhaps remain as ignorant as before of science, yet through this artist the spirit of that scientist will learn all he wishes. The artist may remain as ignorant about science as before, except for some vague idea of scientific discovery which will be felt in the mind of this artist.

Do the souls who have passed from the earth always learn from the earth or do they teach those on the earth? Both, they learn as well as teach.

Are there any spirits who care little for the life they have left behind? Many, among them good ones who are only concerned with the journey onwards. It is those as a rule whose heart, so to speak, is still attached to the life of the earth and in whose heart the interest for the journey onwards has not yet been kindled, it is they who are inclined to keep in communication with this world. There are exceptions; there are spirits who out of kindness to a few or to many wish to still keep in connection with the earth in order to serve and to be useful. But the spirits of the latter kind still go on advancing towards the goal instead of detaining themselves in communicating with the people on the earth.

What connection do the spirits have with the *jinns*, the inhabitants of the *jinn* world? They are as far removed from them as one planet is from the other, yet in the same universe.

Do they ever meet with *jinns,* the inhabitants of that sphere? Yes they do, but only such spirits who are not closed, or imprisoned, or captive in their own world; only those who have gained that strength and power, even while on earth, to break any ropes that bind them and liberate themselves from all situations, however difficult. But how do these brave ones arrive at this stage? By rising above themselves. If this limited self, which makes the false ego, is broken, and one has risen above the limitations of life in all the planes of existence, that soul will break all boundaries and will experience liberation, which is the longing of every soul.

* * *

Question: *You said yesterday that it was better if the soul after passing could throw off all that it had learned while on earth. Surely the spiritual development and wisdom must be valued, even after passing? Or does the soul learn that all over again, and much quicker, and thus lose no time?*

Answer: I doubt whether I have said exactly those same words, "That it was better that the soul. ..." And if I said it, I think it was my mistake. I may have said it in other words, in another capacity.

Question: *Is the soul hindered in its progress by being called back to earth by mediums and sorrowing friends?*

Answer: Certainly. Suppose a person was going from here to Paris, and he had not yet gone as far as that door, and someone calls him, "Please, stop, come here, I miss you." Perhaps he has gone further, and there a person calls, "Please stop, I want to speak to you." It means that he always will be detained, he will never arrive there. Then the purpose for which he was going is hindered. Now it is meant that he must go further. To call him backward, I should think is a fault against nature itself. With all our love and affection, the one whom we love, if it happens that that soul has passed and is going forward, it is better to help that soul to go forward. And that one can do by sending one's loving thought, helping it on to go forward.

It amused me, sometimes people telling me, "I have loved someone so much that I would not like that person to go far, that I might not be able to catch him. Will he stay in the same place until I come?" It is most amusing: to detain a person; if that person was meant to be with another person, he should not have gone! It is for his good. Detaining him would be pulling him back from that progress which is the longing of every soul.

Question: *When the soul coming towards manifestation meets a soul on its return journey, is the latter one aware of the meeting?*

Answer: Not always aware. It depends upon the soul. Are there not in this world many souls who are unaware of any presence? There are other souls who are conscious.

Question: *Do the souls who come to realization here, not go to the* jinn *or angelic world after death, but straight back to God?*

Answer: But it is the same way; they go by the same way, the way they came, that is the way to God. But the ones who go to God, they do not stop here. Even on the earth, they can go to God, not be on the earth. To go to God one need not go through death. Crucifixion is the condition. They can go to God even from here. For God is nearer to them than any sphere of angels or anything else. Even to the *jinn* world, it is perhaps a journey of one step; to the angelic world, two steps. But to go to God, no step. He is there; if one were only conscious, he is there.

Now I also can say about this question: Is the last, or the highest stage that the soul perceives, is that stage attained without experiencing the *jinn* world? I should say yes, but there is no joy in it. The joy of life is the joy in the journey. If one closed one's eyes and was immediately put on the top of the Himalayas, one would not enjoy it so much as the one who would climb and see the different scenery, and meet with different people, and breathe the different atmosphere and air. That is the joy of it. If one were put there with closed eyes, one would be frightened. The whole joy is of the journey.

Question: *Are there in the* jinn *and angelic worlds the opportunities for the souls to do the same things as they were busy with on the earth? How can that be?*

Answer: That can be. Nothing is impossible. Why must it not be?

Question: *Is it not possible that souls on the other side may wish to communicate with some on earth who have no faith or conviction of the truth and reality of the spiritual world? How can this conviction be given?*

Answer: There are many souls who communicate with the people on the earth, but the people on the earth do not clearly receive their communications. But at the same time unconsciously they receive them. And very often they do errands, thinking that they are doing them of their free will, or because they wish to do it; really speaking, they are doing an errand for a spirit gone beyond. And in order to give a conviction to a person of the world above, why must spirits strive; why must man not develop his faith? And if man is so obstinate as to keep away from developing himself, he will keep the same obstinacy in the other world. So the angels need not come to wake him. For in man is the possibility of faith. The interference of the *jinn* world is not necessary.

Question: *Do spirits see the mental bodies on earth the same as they see one another?*

Answer: Certainly they do.

Question: *Do they have day and night, sunrise and sunset?*

Answer: Certainly they have.

Question: *Do they have forms and factories?*

Answer: Certainly, all things that you have here, you have there, made exactly on the same model.

40

THE SOUL, which functions on its way to manifestation in different bodies, covering itself thus with one body over another body, has a power which it uses to a smaller or greater degree in the renewing of the tissues of the body and in healing it. The child born in the family in which there are physical infirmities is often born already healed and with tissues renewed. The reason is because the soul is the divine breath; it purifies, revivifies, and heals the instrument in which it functions.

On its return journey the soul shows the same phenomenon in a different way. From all the impressions of illness, of sadness, of miseries which the soul had experienced while on the earth and had taken into the spirit world, it heals its being and renews the tissues of that body which still remains with it after having left the physical body. It purifies it from all illness and its impressions, and thus renews its life in the spirit world in accordance to its evolution. But, apart from evolution, it is the tendency of the soul to repel all that is foreign to it, either from the physical body or from the mental body, which it still has in the spirit world.

The soul is on a continual journey; in whatever plane, it is journeying all the time and in this journey it has a purpose to accomplish, many purposes contained and hidden in one purpose. There are objectives which remain unfulfilled in one's lifetime on the earth. They are accomplished in the further journey in the spirit world. For nothing that the human heart has once desired remains unfulfilled. If it is not fulfilled here, it is accomplished in the hereafter. The desire

217

of the soul is the wish of God, small or great or right or wrong, and it has a moment of fulfilment. If that moment does not come while the soul is on the earth plane, it comes in its further journey in the spirit world.

The soul proves its divine origin in all planes of existence, wherever it happens to pass, in creating for itself all it desires, in producing for itself its heart's object, in gratifying itself with all it wishes, and in attracting and drawing to itself all it wants. The source of the soul is perfect and so is its goal. Therefore, even through its limitation the soul has a spark of perfection. The nature of perfection is: no want. Even as it is limitation that the soul experiences on the earth, where it lives the life of limitation, still its one desire is perfection, to achieve and obtain all that it wants, so this want is supplied for the very reason that the perfect One, even in the world of variety, does everything possible to experience perfection.

* * *

Question: *Do children who die as infants come to maturity, and on which plane? The angelic or the* jinn?

Answer: Yes, they do; often on the *jinn* plane, and sometimes in the plane of the angels. It depends upon the quality of the soul and upon the object it was meant to accomplish.

Question: *Is there then no illness or impression of illness on the* jinn *plane?*

Answer: Yes, there is. As there are illnesses in the human plane, on the plane of the earth, so there are certain discomforts on the other plane. But in telling you the healing power of the soul, I have explained that it heals the body that it functions in, even on the earth. And the illness that it takes from the earth, it heals again in the hereafter. No doubt, the discomforts of that plane still remain, for life is a continual struggle. The struggle there is more easy to combat, for the reason that the facilities of the other plane are greater, as the limitations of this plane are great.

Question: *If a soul desires wrong or cruel things, how can that be a wish of God?*

Answer: To the person who has asked me this question, I will ask, "Why did God make a person desirous of wrong wishes?"

Question: *Can souls by evil thinking and doing deliberately kill their spirits, and so perish?*

Answer: No, they only cover themselves by the clouds of ignorance, which cause discomfort. But no soul perishes. The soul is not meant to perish.

Question: *You said, "The desire of the soul is the wish of God, small or great, right or wrong." How can the wish of God be wrong?*

Answer: There are many things for which man accuses God of having done wrong. It is only out of his respect to God that he does not say anything. I think there is no person in the world who can be accused so many times for wrong-doing as God. The reason is that it is our limited self that judges, which is not capable of judging.

Question: *You once said that this message would teach the laboring men to make from the labor their way of meditation. Will you please speak more on this subject?*

Answer: By this I meant that the chief work of this message is to make the everyday life of man a religion, his profession his religion, his work his religion. Whatever he is capable of doing, he must do it. And at the same time, while doing it, he can meditate on the same work by knowing the secret meaning of that work which he is doing, and in this way turn his life, the same life, from worldly life into spiritual life. From everything he is qualified to do, and which he is needed to do, while doing it, he will be accomplishing his religion and attaining spirituality by his meditation on the evolution of his work, however uninteresting his work, as soon as he knows how to do the meditation rightly.

Whether a person is doing gardening or factory work, as

soon as he knows the meditation of the work he is doing, every work will become a meditation for him. Yesterday I was envying a fisherman, sitting there. Looking at that fisherman, who was sitting with patience and peace, and yet making his efforts to get the fish, I thought, "What a place of meditation, sitting in the woods near the water." Of course the man in the factory has not that facility. Nature is bliss. Still for the man in the factory, his wages will be nothing compared with the bliss he gets if he knows meditation. Now it is a loss; by that he is gaining what he gains, but at the same time [he loses].

What will happen when the initiated ones, some of the mureeds who have an interest in the factory or the trades, when they will have the leading of the thing? Then they will be giving the message at the factory. There is no other thing to think about; when the right teaching is given, a person will work even better than other people because his mind will be concentrated.

My own experience is this: I came to the station of Rajputan; I had to send a telegram. There I saw a man who was busy with his telegraphic work and at the same time he was doing his meditation. It interested me very much, a man so busy as that, who had to listen every time to the bell and do the work. A mistake of one letter and he would have been held responsible. He came to me and I said, "I have come to give you this telegram. But I marvel at you." I said, "It is wonderful how you are keeping your concentration during this work." He smiled instantly, and we became friends, and had a very interesting talk afterwards. But if not, the spiritual work would be a nuisance. And especially in such times when the needs of life are so great that everybody has a certain work to do, and they have very few hours of rest. And if a person meditates only once in a week, or if a person thinks that after he reaches a certain age he will have leisure, then the whole life is wasted. The best method, therefore, is to use the way of meditation in one's everyday life. Whatever one does must be done with meditation. One will not only have the benefit from earth, but also from heaven. The benefit will be a thousand times greater.

Question: *What is meditation?*

Answer: Meditation means the soul's action towards spiritual unfoldment. And this endeavor may be practiced in different ways, in order to suit one's own profession and work.

41

In THE SOUL'S coming on earth and its return, in both there is a process to be seen. When coming on earth, it adorns itself with the covers of the particular planes through which it passes, and on its return it uncovers itself from the bodies it has adopted for the convenience of experiencing that particular plane. In this way it is a process of covering and uncovering. The soul, so to speak, throws off its garment in the same plane from which it borrowed it when it has no more to do with it. Then what happens to these bodies?

The earthly bodies are composed of physical atoms, and so all that has been composed becomes decomposed and turns into its own element: the air to air, the heat to the fire, water to water, and earth to the earth. In spite of all the diverse aspects that the body apparently may have absorbed—many insects may eat it, birds may share it in their food, and animals such as the lion may swallow it, or it may be eaten by a fish, one fish or many fishes, or it may turn into soil in time, or be used to strengthen a tree or plants—in every case the first rule remains.

Just as a physical body composes and decomposes, so does the mental body or spirit body, a body which has incomparably longer life than the physical body has on the earth. Its end is similar to the end of the physical body. When the soul uncovers itself from this mental garb, it falls as flat as the body of the earth, in that plane in which it belongs. For it is not the body which has the strength to stand; the strength of standing belongs to the soul. It is therefore that man, in whom the soul manifests in a most pronounced form, stands upright, all other animals bowing and bending naturally by their natural form.

Is the decomposing of the spirit body used in making the bodies there? Certainly it is. Not in such a crude way as it happens with the earthly body, but in a much finer way, for this is a finer body. There is a joy in the composing and decomposing of this body, as there is even a pleasure in the composing and decomposing of the physical body. The question is, "What does the body that the soul has look like in the spirit plane?" It looks exactly the same as when one was on the earth. But why should there not be a change? Why must it be so? Because of man's love for his body. Does it change? Yes, if he wishes it to change. If the soul wishes it to be changed, it can be changed to its own ideal. It can be made as young and as beautiful as possible, but it must be remembered that by nature the soul becomes so attached to its form, that it holds on to it. It does not like to become different as a rule.

The condition of the next world is most like the condition of the dream world. In the dream one does not see oneself much different from the way one appears except in some cases and at some times, and for that there are reasons. Nevertheless, the power that the soul has in the next world is much greater than it has in this world of limitations. The soul in the other world, so to speak, matures and finds within itself the power of which it was ignorant through life, the power of creating and producing all it wishes through life. And its movements not being hindered so much by time and space, it is more capable of doing for itself and of accomplishing things which are difficult for the same soul to do and accomplish on the earth plane.

* * *

Question: *Is there a compensation for a being with a soul craving for expression in art, music, etc., and who is yet bound to strive a long life of drudgery?*

Answer: Certainly there is. If it were not so, there would not be justice. What is not gained in this life is accomplished in the next. Therefore, there is a scope for hope throughout life.

Question: *Is the person who definitely communes many hours a day with God closer to him than he who must concentrate on his duties, without chance of communing definitely?*

Answer: One must make one's duties a religion and find a means of communication through one's everyday life. If the Sufi message has anything to bring to the world, it is this. By the meditations and concentrations which are given to the mureeds, it is not meant that this is the only means for them to communicate with God. That is a way, that is a key. From that way they must develop and learn to communicate with God in all things that they do in their life. It is not sufficient to sit for half an hour or an hour in the thought of God. Every moment of our life must be devoted to it.

I remember the words of my Murshid answering my question on sin and virtue. He said, "There is one sin, and one virtue. The moment which is passed in the absence of God is the sin, and every moment in life which is passed in the presence of God is virtue." In the whole working in the Sufi culture, its object is that we must arrive at a stage in our life, after learning this way of concentration, that every moment of our life we are in communion with God. When we are talking with others, when we are walking, sleeping, in every action we do, God must be before us.

Question: *Is that in everyone's reach?*

Answer: We are meant to that. Just think, when a person is in love with someone, he is capable of doing it. He thinks of that same person all the time; while eating, drinking, or walking, the image of the beloved is there. That shows that man is capable of it. When the same love is developed for God, it is natural to think of God at every moment of our life, in all we do.

Question: *Do souls on the mental plane retain the memory and knowledge of their experience on the earth?*

Answer: Retain? They are engraved by it. It is just like a white cloth which has its colors and impressions and all that

225

is printed upon it. It is printed with it. With this it has made its world. The soul comes alone, but goes with a world with it. And really speaking, the soul would have liked to have taken the earthly body if it could. But it is not allowed there; therefore, it has to leave it here.

Question: *Are there courtship and marriages, and are children born on the mental plane?*

Answer: It is not necessary that the law of the spiritual plane should work so much in accordance with the law of the physical plane. Even on the physical plane the law differs. Among the living creatures there are egg-born and other different creatures. Then there are living creatures who are born out of the animal world, who come from the leaf, from the fruit—quite a different process. When there are such varieties here, so the laws of the spirit world must not be compared exactly with the law of this world. Still, one law remains all through, in all planes, and that is the law of duality, negative and positive, the law of expression and conception; every issue, in whichever plane, comes subject to this law.

Question: *How can the belief in God and the conviction of his existence and reality be brought home to those who have none?*

Answer: We must not trouble much about it. We must be concerned with ourselves because there is so much to be done with ourselves. When once God becomes a reality in ourselves, then we have a living God to give to the other. One person speaks of gold; the other has gold coins, he can give them. When our belief has become living, it must have an influence upon others; it cannot fail, it will not fail.

Question: *Do the personalities of unevolved souls, such as those of primitive natives, and those sunk in materialism, persist through death?*

Answer: Certainly, they all do. Every soul that has wakened on the earth has a next station to make before it starts for the next world and that station is the spirit world. Not only human beings, but this also applies to all living creatures.

Question: *When the soul decomposes its bodies after using them, does the matter of the decomposed body thus used by man do anything to lift the matter of the planes it returns to?*

Answer: Yes, matter evolves, and used by the higher entities it evolves still. But the nature of evolution is different. For instance, matter as a whole is evolving to a much better condition and is more fresh than matter which has gone into it again and been taken by it. But at the same time this aspect of evolution is different from the general evolution of matter.

Question: *Is there an advantage for the animal when it is used as food for man?*

Answer: It is not an advantage for the animal, but it is an advantage for the whole. All that is absorbed by man, in the way of eating, whether fruit or flower, is all blessed, because in man the soul has reached its ultimate state. Therefore, to give that soul an experience, or pleasure, or life, or strength, or satisfaction, whatever is used, it is all used for its best purpose, for it is used for the best expression of the soul. Of course, when a person stands on another level, he can see it from another point of view. From that point of view he may see the justice or injustice of it. But from this point of view it has its reason also.

Question: *"There is a pleasure in the composing and decomposing of the physical body." What do you mean by this?*

Answer: I will answer by the example of a drunken man: he knows that he drinks alcohol, which is poison. It is killing the germs [cells?] of his body and blood, and doing him all harm. And yet that decomposing is the very reason that gives him the joy of drinking. It is the dying process which gives him the joy. It is gradual dying which is his pleasure. And it will amuse you that I once asked a drunken man, "Oh, why are you doing this drinking all the time? What are you killing yourself for!" "I do not care, I would rather die than not drink!" Because it is the pleasure of dying. There is a pleasure in dying.

42

THE SOUL who has passed from the earth and is in the spirit world can live on the earth in one way, and that way is the transmigration of the soul. Very often people have wrongly explained this idea when they have said that a spirit takes hold of a dead body, and entering into it, makes use of it. The body once dead is dead. It is in the process of returning to its own origin. It has lost that magnetism which attracts the soul and holds it in order to allow it to function in the physical body. If the dead body had the magnetism, then it would not have allowed the soul to return; it would have held it back, for it is the body which holds the soul towards the earth, the soul which has a pull from within, drawing it continually towards its source.

But there are many living dead, in the good sense or the bad sense of the word. It is in these cases that a single-pointed spirit takes hold of their minds and bodies as its own instruments, using them to its best advantage. It is this which is generally known as obsession. In point of fact, there is no soul who has not experienced obsession in the true sense of the word. For there are moments in one's everyday life when those on the other side take the souls on the earth as their medium to experience life on the earth. Transmigration of the soul makes a much deeper impression upon the soul than what obsession might give. For in time, the spirit who enters into the being of a person on earth makes the person entirely void of himself. In time he loses his identity and becomes one with the spirit who has obsessed him. Not only in his thought, speech and action, but also in his attitude and outlook, in his habits and manners, even in his looks he becomes like the entity which obsesses him.

Might one say then it is a good thing from a mystical point of view to become thus selfless? No, that is not the way of being selfless. In this way one is robbed of the self. The mystical way of being selfless is meant to realize the self by unveiling the self of the numberless covers of the false ego.

* * *

Question: *Is it a great lack in character when a person cannot give the love which friends require? To receive love and be unable to return it, to have forgotten friends while absorbed in one's work and occupation?*

Answer: The question is what work or occupation? There are works and occupations which are of a higher character, which take one's whole attention, one's life. And such work may require renunciation and sacrifice. Then one does not become loveless; it is duty. One cannot be regardless. But if one can manage to give and take love at the same time, it is preferable.

Question: *Will a person suffer one day through inability to love, merely giving a cool affection?*

Answer: Love, whether hot or cold, is love. Is there cold love? Since God is love, the whole manifestation is love, the cold water or the hot water.

Question: *Is it not a pity that a person who is gifted cannot bring out his talent and it remains hidden?*

Answer: No, that person must do his best to come out in the world and express the art and literature he is capable of. He must not keep it back: "Raise your light on high"; all that is in the heart, bring it out. If the conditions are against you, come through it. That is the struggle of life. In order to make life a success, one must make a part of life like a soldier's, to struggle along, to make it out.

Question: *Which is the power by which man attracts his food to him and the things he needs so that his wishes are granted? Is it by his God realization, consciously or unconsciously?*

Answer: If there is any power which is a mighty power, it is the power of love. All that one desires is also love. Even if one desires food, it is the love of food. All that one desires, it is the love of it. And it is according to the power of love that one will attract. Only what does one love more, something more than the ordinary things of life? Then that must be one's aim.[44]

Question: *Shall we see the great being of Christ and come nearer to him in the other worlds?*

Answer: Certainly.

Question: *What was the lesson of the raising of Lazarus*[45] *from the dead? And why are we told, if we had faith we could raise the dead?*

Answer: Explanations of miracles, and especially of the great ones, are difficult to make—for the sake of the idea of the people, to preserve the faith of people who believe in them. It has a symbolical side, which is the interesting part of the story, that in spite of the sisters being interested, the brother remains the same. Dead is he; with his ears open and his eyes open, he cannot see and hear. That person is more dead than a person in his grave. The stone was the stone over his own thought, which was the hindrance for him to see. When the moment came that a new life might be brought to his soul, that his soul should see the Christ and his message, when such a moment came, then the Master came, and then his heart was melted. And that life which was to spring up, sprang. That is the real miracle, in an even greater sense than the outer miracle.

43

THE SOUL, on its way towards the goal in the spheres of *jinn*, has some riches collected during its life on the earth, in the form of merits, qualities, experience and convictions, talents, attitude, and a certain outlook on life. In spite of the belongings of the earth which it has returned to the earth on its passing, this soul in the spirit world offers these riches, allows them to be taken from it, and imparts them to the souls coming from their source who are on their way to the earth.

The souls on their way to the earth, full of heavenly bliss but poor in earthly riches, purchase the current coin of the earth in the *jinn* plane. Guarantees and contracts and mortgages and all the accounts that the spirit had left un-finished on the earth, they have taken on as their charge to pay or to receive when coming on the earth. Among these souls who come on the earth, there are some who take from one spirit all they can as their heritage from the spirit world, some from many. Yet such souls who absorb, attract, con-ceive and receive all that is given to them in the spirit plane, they have perhaps more of the gift of one spirit than all the other gifts they have from the different spirits they have met.

Does this exchange rob the spirit on its way to the goal of its merits and qualities? No, not in the least. The riches that the soul can take to the spheres of the *jinn* are safe and secure. Any knowledge or learning, merit or talent given to another person is not lost by the person who gives. It only makes the giver richer still.

When the Hindus said in the ancient times to a wicked person, "The next time when you are born, you will come as a dog or a monkey," it was to tell him, who did not know the end of life except through himself, that he might know that his qualities will come again and will bring him back again in a still worse form than what he was before. When they said, "Your good actions will bring you back as a better person, as a higher person," it was in this sense, that the man who did not know the two extreme poles of his soul would understand that no good action was to be lost. And the man who had no hope in the hereafter, as he did not know what it was, and only knew of life to be a life on the earth, for that man it was a consolation to know that all the good that he had done was coming back. And in this sense, the theory is true which is explained in this.

It is only a matter of words, of a difference of words. The soul who comes from above has no name or form, has no particular identity. It makes no difference to that soul what it is called; since it has no name, it could just as well adopt the name of the coat which was put on it, as that is the nature of life. The robe of justice put on a person makes him a judge, and the uniform of a policeman makes him a constable. Neither was the judge born as a judge nor the constable a policeman. They were born on earth nameless if not formless. Distinctions and differences belong to the lower world, not to the higher; therefore, the conception of the Sufi has no argument against the idea of reincarnation. The difference is only in words, and it is necessary that a precaution may be taken that the door may be kept open before souls who wish to enter the kingdom of God, that they may not feel bound by a dogma, that they will have to be dragged back after having left the earth plane by their *karma*.

The soul of man is the spark of God. Though God is helpless on the earth, still he is all-powerful in heaven, and by teaching the prayer, "Thy kingdom come, thy will be done on earth as in heaven," the Master has given a key to every soul who will repeat this prayer, a key to open that door wherein is the secret of almighty power and perfect wisdom, which raises the soul above all limitations.

* * *

Question: *Would it be possible, instead of sending the spirit of a criminal into the spirit world to spread its wickedness, to take precautions so as to lessen the power of that wickedness?*

Answer: Such a punishment purifies. Suffering purifies a person from sin. Life is dear, more so to a material person than to a spiritual person. Therefore, his pain is great. And that pain comes as a rescue for his spirit.

Question: *What do you mean, that God is helpless on earth, but all-powerful in heaven?*

Answer: For the very reason that God is divided in the world into different personalities. In heaven he remains in one personality, then all his power is in one. But his object in all the limited personalities which are on the earth is the same as in heaven, that his will be done. Therefore, every person whether poor or rich, has the wish, "My wish be done." Whose desire is it? God's desire. This desire can only be fulfilled if he would give up his desire to the desire of God. Only on one condition: If he can give up his self for the self of God. That is the meaning of Abraham's sacrifice of his son.[46] And that is the true meaning of crucifixion: give up the false self for the self of God. Then there is perfection, that his will is done. The soul is God's will when he has given up his own will. Then he is the will of God.

Question: *Are there no distinctions and differences on the mental plane?*

Answer: Certainly there are. But the higher we go, the less there is difference and distinction.

Question: *Please tell us if you think capital punishment is wrong?*

Answer: Could you ask Murshid to tell you anything is wrong? Does Murshid say anything is wrong? Nothing.

Question: *Do you think capital punishment is good?*

Answer: If there is no wrong, how can there be good? All is perfect.

Question: *Can a soul on its downward journey receive bad qualities as well as good qualities from returning souls on the* jinn *plane?*

Answer: Certainly, both. How can there be light without shade? It is the light and shade which make the picture complete.

Question: *They have a certain choice?*

Answer: Yes. Every step they take and every impression they receive become the guide to their further step. For instance, when we are walking in a forest, and we do not know the way, we only walk by the inspiration from all we see; so we go. So is the impression of the soul from the place where it starts. It always goes, hearing that music, towards where the music comes from; all the vibrations and beauty, all it has become accustomed to, it goes and receives it. For instance, if all people were fond of good music, no one would go and hear the jazz band. But it seems there are more who are fond of the jazz band. It has become a society custom to go to operas. It is very good that it has been made a custom. They go because they pay more there. If that were not the thing, then very few people would go. If that is the case, then everyone is attracted to that beauty which particularly appeals to his mind. The mind has beforehand a preparation which makes it appreciate that.

Question: *How does the soul move through the planes?*

Answer: In the first place it begins with music. The soul does not know whether it is a false note or a true one. It is the rhythm and tone of a particular soul in accordance to the mysticism of sound. The next step: the same beauty outwardly. In this way it goes on. These three stages, the *jinn*, the human, and the angelic planes, I have spoken of for the facility of my mureeds, just as there are seven notes musicians have given for the facility of those who want to study music. But are there seven notes? No, there are as many as you can create and perceive. It is the limitation of our senses; finer than that we cannot perceive. It is only the grades of a distinction which are perceptible; so these planes are perceptible. But there is one life running through all, there is no gap between, except that there are walls to divide. What are these walls? They are in our perception, because we are unable to go beyond them in reality.

Dividing is for our understanding, because we compare everything with our condition. If we had no rhythm to our pulse, and if we had no breath, we would never have perceived time. If it is finer, it is difficult to perceive. We can only perceive to a certain extent. For instance, the musicians in India have four quarter tones between two notes. The mystics could realize that there are four quarter notes. But is it finished with four? No, there could be a thousand according to the power of our senses. But in reality life is from God to the earth, and from the earth to God. One single stream of life, running through. What do we call this space? We may say it is empty, but is it empty? Our eyes are so limited that we can only see a certain thickness of substance. If it is not so thick, we cannot see it. We call it "nothing." It is not nothing; it is something out of which all things come.

44

DOES THE SPIRIT impart its merits, talents, experience, and knowledge to the new–coming soul, passing through the spirit plane to the earth, consciously or unconsciously? Sometimes it imparts this consciously, in some cases unconsciously, but in the conscious action there is the greatest pleasure for the spirit. For this soul, which is taking the knowledge from a spirit as its heritage from the world of the *jinn,* is considered by the spirit as a child by his parents or a pupil by his teacher. In the heritage of this soul there is a great joy for that spirit.

Do they keep a connection in any way? No connection except a sympathetic link, for one goes to the north while the other goes to the south, one ascending to heaven, the other descending to the earth. A connection or an attachment between them would do nothing but hinder the progress of both.

A soul lives in the spirit world while it is busy accomplishing the purpose of its life, which may last for thousands of years. Does a soul in the spirit world continue to do the same work which it did during its life on the earth? Yes, it does in the beginning, but it is not bound to the same work for this reason, that it is not subject to limitations as it was while on the earth. The soul eventually rises to that standard which was the standard of its ideal. It does that work which was its desire. Are there difficulties in the spirit world as on the earth in doing something and in accomplishing something? Certainly there are, but not so many as here on the earth.

But if there were one object that was desired by various

239

spirits, how can they all attain to it? Will they all get some particles of that object? And if it be a living being, what about it? The law of that world is different from this world of limitations. There souls will find in abundance all which is scarcely to be found here on earth. The picture of this spirit world is given in the story of Krishna. The Gopis[47] of Vandravana all requested young Krishna to dance with them. Krishna smiled and answered each one, "On the evening of the full moon." On the evening of the full moon, all the Gopis gathered in the Vandravana and a miracle happened: as many Gopis as were there, so many Krishnas there were.

The spirit world is incomprehensible to the mind which is only acquainted with the laws of the physical world. An individual who is a limited being here is as a world there. A soul is a person here and a planet there. When one considers the helplessness of this plane, one cannot for a single moment imagine the facility, the convenience, the comfort as the possibilities of the next world. And it is human nature, that all which is not known to man, even with all its greatness and riches, means nothing to him.

A pessimist came to Ali and said, "Is there really a hereafter for which you are preparing us, so we refrain from things of our desire and live a life of goodness and piety? What if there were no such thing as a hereafter?" Ali answered, "If there is not such a thing as a hereafter, I will be in the same boat as you, and if there is a hereafter, then I will be the gainer and you will be the loser." Life lives and death dies; the one who lives will live, must live—there is no alternative.

* * *

Question: *Has it ever happened that a soul which had meant to go forward to the physical plane remained in the sphere of the* jinn *for the love of a soul there?*

Answer: It does happen very often. It is love that takes one forward in one's progress, and again it is love sometimes which changes one from progress. It is only the difference of a higher love. A higher love always takes one forward. When the love is not high enough, it has not the power to go forward. And sometimes it pins one to the same point where one stands. Love is the battery which should be used to go forward.

Question: *Could a soul also persuade a soul who was meant to stay in the* jinn *plane to go with it to earth?*

Answer: As a soul has individualized itself in a certain plane, it becomes the inhabitant of that certain plane; it does not go forward. It stops as long as it wishes to stop, or as long as it is meant to stop, which is thousands of years of this earthly plane. It can go quicker. It is possible, like a person who wishes to finish his life here on the earthly plane, so it is possible there also.

Question: *In "The Soul Towards Manifestation," it is said that* jabrut *is the world of the angels, and in the book* The Message of Spiritual Liberty *it is said that* jabrut *is the astral world. How can we understand this?*

Answer: The angelic plane is the astral plane and *jabrut* is the word for both.

Question: Jabrut *is translated by "astral plane" and* ajsam *is also translated by "astral plane." What are the differences?*

Answer: The only difference is that one is in the sleeping state and the other is the waking state, but it is the same plane.

Question: Lahut *is called spirit and* arwah *is called spirit. What are the differences?*

Answer: *Arwah* is that spirit which has concentrated its light and *lahut* is the attainment of a certain spiritual realization known to the meditating soul.

Question: *Is there belief and disbelief in the spiritual plan? Would not an unbeliever in immortality be convinced of his error by physical death?*

Answer: He would be looking forward to death there; still

he has the impression that there is a death. The one who will not be convinced, no one can convince him of anything.

Question: *As what do the souls who are spiritually evolved live in the hereafter?*

Answer: As planets: as large as they are here, so large a planet they will be there. In the Old Testament one reads that the earth was made first, and the heavens afterwards. Plainly speaking, it is the souls as planets who will form the cosmos there in the spiritual world. Therefore, it was the heaven or the cosmos that was dependent upon the creation of the earth to make the cosmos there perfect.

Question: *How do the souls coming out get impressions from the souls coming back from the earth?*

Answer: They absorb, conceive, learn, and receive all that is given to them by the souls coming from the earth. But what mostly happens is reflection, the reflection of the souls coming from the earth falling upon the souls coming from heaven—becoming impressed. Just like an impression becomes impressed upon the photographic plate, so the photographic plate is developed, and when on the earth the photo is finished.

Question: *Are there in the spirit plane different languages, races, nations?*

Answer: There are as many races and nationalities as on the earth, and war and battles and peace. Each earth has its separate heaven.

Question: *Will there be silence on the* jinn *plane?*

Answer: Yes, silence is a necessity, just as sleep. Where there is an activity, there is a repose. Silence is a reaction to work, and that must be there. But at the same time there will be action just the same. The speed of action will be incomparably greater than the speed of action on the earth.

Question: *Shall we not take our worries there, as we do now into the peace of nature?*

Answer: Yes, just the same.

Question: *What is the Sufi's idea of expansion compared with the Yogi's?*

Answer: The way of the Yogi is to work in order to dive deep within himself, and so pass through all the different planes which stand between himself and God, the Self within. The way of the Sufi, therefore, is the way of expansion; as he draws within, so he widens his outlook on life. So that in the end when he has touched his innermost being, by that time he has embraced almost all that is living. And it is this idea which is pictured by the sign of cross. Reaching one's innermost being is signified by the perpendicular line, and the expansion which widens one's outlook on life is signified by the horizontal line. Therefore, the cross in the end becomes the heart—round. For the circle does not show the two aspects in their essence as the heart shows it. When you look at the center of the heart, it shows the perpendicular line to the mind with keen imagination, and also it gives an idea of the horizontal line. The difference between the circle and the heart is that the circle which expresses the cross is the heart. Therefore, the leaves are heart-shaped rather than round. And the veins of the leaves show the cross.

The Yogi's attitude is keeping away, keeping everyone at a distance. He will bless, but he will bless a person from a distance, and say kindly, "Do not come near." He does not hate, but he would rather be left alone. The Sufi comes with open arms to welcome all who come. For in every person he sees the spark, the divine being. Therefore, he becomes all embracing; in this way he widens his outlook.

45

LIFE IN THE SPHERES of the *jinns* is the phenomenon of mind. The mind is not the same there, with all the thoughts and imaginations which it carries from the earth to this plane. Mind is a mind here, and the whole being there. Thoughts are imaginations here, but reality there. One thinks here, but the same action there, instead of a thought, becomes a deed. For action, which here depends upon the physical body, there becomes the act of the mind.

There is a picture of this idea in a story:[48] There was a man who had heard of there being a tree of desires. He was once traveling and happened to come under the shade of a tree, which was cooling and restful and which made him sit there, leaning against it. He said to himself, "How beautiful is nature here, how cooling is the shade of this tree, and the breeze, most exhilarating. If only I had a soft carpet to sit on and some cushions to lean against." No sooner had he thought about it, than he saw himself sitting in the midst of soft cushions. "How wonderful," he thought, "to have got it." But now he thought, "If there were a glass of cooling drink," and there came a fairy with the glass of cold drink, most delicious. He enjoyed it, but he said, "I would like a dinner, a good dinner." No sooner had he thought of a dinner, than a golden tray was brought to him, with beautifully arranged dishes of all sorts. Now he thought, "If only I had a chariot, then I might take a drive into the forest." A four horse chariot was already there, coachmen greeting him with bent heads. He thought, "Everything I desire comes without any effort. I wonder if it is true or all a dream." No sooner had he thought this, than everything there disappeared, and he found himself sitting on the same ground leaning against the tree.

This is the picture of the spirit world; it is the world of the optimist. The pessimist has no share in its great glory for the reason that he refuses to accept the possibility which is the nature of life, thereby denying to himself all his desires and the possibility of achieving his desires. The pessimist stands against his own light and mars his own object here, and more so in the hereafter, where desire is the seed which is sown on the soil of the spirit world. And optimism is the water which rears the plant. But knowledge at the same time gives that sunshine which helps the plants to flourish on the earth as well as in the spheres of the *jinns*.

Is there a death for the spirits in the spheres of the *jinns*? Yes, they have it, but after a much longer time, a death not so severe as on the earthly plane, where everything is crude and coarse, but a change which is slightly felt after a long life, after the fulfillment of every desire. What causes their death? Is there illness or disease? Yes, there are discomforts or pains peculiar to that plane, not to be compared to the plane of the earth.

What especially brings about death in the sphere of the *jinns* is the moment when hope gives way and there is no more ambition there. It is the loss of enthusiasm which is a death there and the cause of death here on the earth. The souls in the spirit world have more control of their life and death than those on the earth. The world of the spirit is his own world, it is a planet. When it loses the strength and magnetism which hold the soul functioning in it, it falls like a star from heaven and the soul departs to its own origin.

* * *

Question: *When several souls are impressed by the same soul, do they recognize themselves when on earth, and do they resemble each other in mind and character?*

Answer: They do resemble each other as the children of the same parents do, and yet they are different, as brothers and sisters differ from one another. They are attracted to one another, and they find their thoughts and ideas akin to each other. Also, they show this nearness in the similarity of their work.

Question: *Does it take a soul coming towards manifestation a long time to get the impression from souls coming back? Is the impression imparted instantly? And if not, is it like taking lessons with someone, as we do on the earth?*

Answer: No, as a rule the reflection is just like a photographic plate. The difference is of the quality of the soul. There is one soul upon which the impression instantly is made. There is another soul which takes time to take the impression. That is because of the intensity of power and the radiance that the soul itself brings with it. It is like the children born on the earth. There are some who are intelligent, who are quick to perceive and willing to learn. There are others unwilling to learn and not quick in their perception.

Question: *How do we see the love of God in the book of nature? We see all around fruits and plants and animal life brought to fruition and then destroyed. And among men cruelty and misery and tragedies and enemy qualities everywhere.*

Answer: It is the focus, the difference of focus. If we focus our mind upon all that is good and beautiful, we shall see, in spite of all the ugliness that exists in nature, and especially more pronounced in the human, that it will cover itself. We shall spread a cover over it, and we shall see all that is beautiful. And what lacks beauty we shall give to it because of all that is beautiful in us; we can add to it by taking beauty from our own heart where it has been collected sufficiently. But if we focus our mind on all the ugliness that exists in nature and in human nature, there will be much of it; and it will take up all our attention, and there will be a time that we will not be able to see any good anywhere. We shall see all cruelty and ugliness and unkindness everywhere.

Question: *Do the planets of different souls interpenetrate, or are they separate?*

Answer: They are entirely apart, one from the other. But at the same time the law of the cosmic system is the same here and in the next world, for they all hold one another by their power of magnetism, by their power of attraction. And so we, the human beings on earth, attract one another and repel one another, subject to the law of magnetism. Furthermore, like human beings on the earth, each stands apart, and yet we have an influence on one another, and we have friendship and attachment and acquaintance, a connection, a relation. The same can be found in the cosmic system with the planets, and the same law is to be seen in the sphere of the *jinns*.

Question: *In focusing on only the beautiful, is there not a danger of shutting our eyes to the ugliness and suffering we might alleviate?*

Answer: In order to help the poor one ought to be rich. And in order to take away the badness of a person, we ought to be so much more good. And that goodness must be earned, as money is earned. And that earning of goodness is collecting goodness. And if we do not focus on goodness, we shall not be able to collect it sufficiently. What happens is that man becomes agitated against all the absence of goodness that he sees; and being himself poor, he cannot add to it. But unconsciously he develops in his own nature what he sees. He says, "Oh, poor person, I would like you so much to be good." But that does not help. His agitation, his looking to the badness, only adds one more wicked person. When one has focused one's eyes on goodness, one will add to the beauty. But when one's eyes are focused on the bad, one will collect the wickedness sufficiently to add to the number of the wicked in the end. Besides, by criticizing, judging, and by looking at wickedness with contempt, one does not help the wicked, one does not help the stupid. The one who helps is the one who is ready to overlook, who is ready to forgive, to tolerate, to take the disadvantages that one may have to meet with patiently; it is that one who can help.

Question: *As the spirit world brings the fulfillment of every desire, a soul who has died before death will only stay there for a very short time?*

Answer: "Died before death," what do you mean by it? He is the king of this world. And never think that the one who has died before death has no desire. The desire springs up again, only he is not beneath the desire, he is above the desire. The picture of the god Vishnu shows Vishnu sitting upon the lotus. The lotus is desire, every petal. Sitting upon it does not mean that he does not possess them. But they are under him instead of being over his head.

Question: *Does the length of the time the spirit remains in the plane of the* jinn *depend on the life on earth?*

Answer: Not necessarily. But to some extent there is a relation, because it is what one takes from the life of the earth, according to the largeness of his life. If a person has stayed on the earth for a shorter time, the duration of his stay in the world of *jinns* will be less. But at the same time there is another condition, and that is: the one who has stayed less here has much more to accomplish there than the one who has stayed longer here. This is to be taken more in a spiritual sense. For him it is not a necessity that he should stay there long, unless it is his desire. But in the case of the other [condition], it is necessary for him to stay there longer to accomplish his task.

Question: *You said, "That world brings the fulfillment of every desire." Also of those desires which are called passions?*

Answer: Of every desire. But the tree of passions is raised, only not in the same sense as it is on the earth.

Question: *Is there the difference in the* jinn *sphere that there we shall see our goal and have hope, while here it is dark?*

Answer: Yes, for the possibilities of the sphere of the *jinn* are greater than we have here on the earth, owing to the limitations caused by the earthly life.

249

Question: *What is the physical or psychical effect of the falling stars, called shooting stars?*

Answer: The physical [psychical?] effect of the stars is only with souls living on the earth who have any relation or connection, any link with that particular star. Because the falling of that particular star is the falling of that person, the death of the person, or at least failure.

Question: *Do the spirits meet with accidents, or are they killed?*

Answer: They meet with all sorts of experience, as they do on the earth.

Question: *When a spirit dies, do those who stand around it sorrow over it?*

Answer: Certainly they do, not so much perhaps as on the earth.

Question: *Does the planet of each soul have in it just the things which that soul thinks or imagines, or other things also?*

Answer: Just the things which that soul thinks or imagines, and also the things which that soul creates.

46

THE SOUL enters the angelic heavens, and it is allowed to enter the heavens with the same condition as before: it has to leave all that belonged to the sphere of the *jinns* in that sphere. Thus, by uncovering itself from the garb of the spirit world, it finds its entrance into the world of the angels. Does it take anything from the world of the angels? Yes, not thoughts, but feelings that it may collect. The life of the soul therefore, in this sphere, is felt more by its vibrations.

Every soul that enters the spheres of the angels vibrates according to what it has gathered during its life in the physical world and in the world of the *jinns*. The example of this is manifested to our view here if we would only observe life more keenly. Every person, before he does anything or says one word, begins to vibrate aloud what he is, what he has done, what he will do. "What you are speaks louder than what you say."

The soul, apart from the body and mind, is a sound, a note, a tone, which is called in Sanskrit *sura*. If this note is inharmonious and has dissonant vibrations, it is called in the Sanskrit language, *asura*: out of tune. The soul therefore, in the heaven of the angels, has not got sins or virtues to show, nor has it a heaven or hell to experience, neither does it show any particular ambition or desire. It is either in tune or out of tune. If it is in tune, it takes its place in the music of the heavens as a note in tune. If it is not in tune, it falls short of it, producing a dissonant effect for itself and for others.

What occupation has the soul there? Its occupation is to be around the light and life, like the bee around the flower. What is its sustenance? Its sustenance is divine light and divine life; divine beauty it sees, divine air it breathes, in the sphere of freedom it dwells, and the presence of God it enjoys.

Life in the sphere of the angels is one single music, one continual music. Therefore it is that the wise of all ages have called music celestial, a divine art. The reason is that the heaven of the angels is all music; in the activity, the repose, and the atmosphere, it is all harmony, continually working towards greater and greater harmony.

What connection has the soul now with the spheres of the *jinn*, once it has arrived in the angelic heavens? No connection necessarily, except a sympathetic link if it happens to have it with anyone there, or if it happens that the body in which it functioned had given way before it had accomplished what it wanted to accomplish.

The joy and happiness of the angelic heavens is so great that the joy of the sphere of the *jinns* cannot be compared with it, and the pleasure of the earth must not even be talked about. For earthly pleasures are mere shadows of that happiness which belongs to the heavens of the angels, and the joy of the sphere of the *jinns* is like the wine that may touch the lips but has never been drunk. That wine one drinks, on arriving at the heavens of the angels, in Sufi terminology is called *kauthar*.

There is a Hindu saying that there are four things which intoxicate the soul: physical energy, wealth, power, and learning; but the intoxication that music gives excels all other forms of intoxication. Then fancy the music of the heavens, where harmony is in its fullness. What happiness that could give, man on earth cannot imagine. If the experience of that music is known to anyone, it is to the wakened soul whose body is here, whose heart is in the spheres of the *jinns* and whose soul is in the heavens of the angels, who while sitting on the earth can experience all the planes of existence. They term the music of the angelic sphere *saut-e-sarmad*, the happiness which carries one to the highest heavens, lifting one from worries and anxieties and from all the limitations of the plane of this earth.

The Soul Towards the Goal

* * *

Question: *How does a soul that is not in tune manage to enter the heavens? Surely it must spoil the harmony for all the others?*

Answer: Yes, that shows that there is even no peace in heaven. The inharmonious people follow the harmonious ones as far as to heaven. But as the soul goes further, it becomes more and more in tune. But at the same time, the vibrations are different; one is more harmonious than the other. But they all fit into the one music of heaven for the reason that in music you do not want all alike, all different notes are necessary.

Question: *Do the souls who are still out of tune after reaching the angelic heavens have a chance of becoming harmonious?*

Answer: There is a chance of harmony at every step, even as far as the heavens and in the heavens. For life is progressive, and therefore there is always hope of improving.

Question: *We often speak of people on earth having guardian angels; is this so, do we each have one?*

Answer: That is quite another thing which has nothing to do with this subject. Yes, those who are one's well wishers are either in the sphere of the *jinn* or in the angelic heaven. If the link of sympathy exists, certainly their light is thrown upon those walking on the earth. Just like the love and good will of the parents, so their love and kindness, forgiveness and good wishes every now and then shines upon the people on the earth and in the spheres of the *jinn*. In short, illuminated souls, wherever they will be, will show their light, in whatever sphere, whatever plane.

Question: *Is it because discord is necessary for harmony sometimes?*

Answer: Not at all. Discord is not necessary for harmony. It can be harmonized; when there are more chords and there is a large part of harmony, then even the dissonant notes

253

can be taken in. They are tuned also, because the note which is a note of discord will come to its perfection. But the answer in a few words is that the soul is continually on the journey towards improvement. Therefore, even in the angelic world the soul is not yet perfect, it is going towards the goal. The perfection is in the goal, not in the soul.

Question: *Is there any difference in the degree of the experience of happiness of the souls going towards manifestation, and those returning?*

Answer: Certainly there is. But this degree is like the difference of notes in music. Particularly the souls returning to the goal have acquired something from the earth and something from the sphere of the *jinn,* which has influenced the tone and the rhythm of their being. And therefore they, so to speak, tell the legend of their past in the music they make in the heavens of the angels.

Question: *Are the small beings that are sometimes seen, called pixies, brownies, little men or the little people, generally elementals?*

Answer: Yes.

47

WHAT BODY has the soul in the heavens of the angels? Though the soul continues in the spheres of the *jinn* with the body in the likeness of the one it had before while on earth, an enormous change takes place in its body and form while in the spheres of the *jinn*. By the time it departs from there, there is hardly any trace left of the body it had in the spheres of the *jinn* and before, for it is turned into a luminous being. Its body is then one of radiance, light itself.

The only difference is that light, as we understand it on the physical plane, is of a different character, for it is visible, but there it is both light and life in one; so the light is audible as well as visible, besides intelligent. One may say, but the physical body is intelligent also. Yes, it is; it is its intelligence which we call sensitiveness. But the body in the sphere of the *jinns* is even more intelligent. And the body that remains in the angelic spheres is more intelligent still. It may be called intelligence itself.

The life of the souls in the angelic spheres is incomparably longer than the life of those on the spheres of the *jinn*. No more desires, no more ambitions, no more strivings have they, only the aspiration to reach further, to experience a greater happiness, a tendency to go on further, closer to that light which is now within their sight. They are flying around this light like the moth around the lantern. The magic lantern, which is the seeking of all souls, is now within their horizon. Nothing else has a greater attraction for them than this light which is continually burning before them. They live and move and make their being[49] in this divine light.

The sizes of bodies in the sphere of the *jinns* and in the heaven of the angels are as numerous as on the earth plane. The size of the body that the soul brings from the sphere of the *jinns* is much larger than the size of the physical body, and the size of the body which adorns the soul from the angelic heavens is larger still. But when the soul dons the body from the sphere of the *jinns*, that body not only covers the physical body, but also enters into it. And so the body brought from the angelic heavens covers both the bodies of the sphere of the *jinns,* as well as of the physical plane, and yet enters into the innermost part of man's being. In this way the angelic and the *jinn* bodies not only surround the physical body, but exist within it. When the soul is on its way to the physical plane, its bodies grow and develop and become more distinct, and as the soul advances toward the goal, its bodies become more ethereal and luminous, but indistinct.

Have they anything to offer to the souls going towards manifestation? Yes, their feelings. In what way do they offer them? The souls coming from the source and going towards the earth are tuned by them, are set to a certain rhythm. It is this offering which determines the line they tread in the future. The Sufis call that day of tuning *roz-e-azl*, the day when the plan was designed for the life of that particular soul. Does one soul impress the new soul coming towards earth with its tune and rhythm, with its feeling and senti-ment? No, not necessarily one soul, even many souls may impress it, but it is the one impression which is dominant.

Is there any link or connection established between the souls who give and take thus, one from the other? Yes, a link of sympathy, a feeling of love and friendliness, an impression of joy which a soul carries with it even to its destination when it comes on the earth. An infant's crying is very often the expression of its longing for the heavens; even the smiles of an infant are a narrative of their memories of heaven and of the spheres above.

Does the soul who meets with the new-coming soul receive anything? It does not require much; it is full of joy in approaching the culmination of life, the goal of its journey. Yet the purity that the new-coming soul brings, with new life and light, gives ease to this soul striving towards the goal and illuminates its path.

There is almost too much that a soul has to do on the earth. There is also much the soul has to accomplish in the spirit world, but there is much less to accomplish in the heavens of the angels. For as the soul proceeds forward, so its burden becomes lighter. The only condition of proceeding forward and drawing closer to the goal is by throwing away the heavy burden which the soul has taken upon itself through its journey. If one might say that the soul lives thousands of years in the sphere of the *jinns*, it is millions of years that one can say, for the convenience of expression, that the soul passes in the heavens of angels, until there comes the moment when the soul is most willing to depart even from that plane of love, harmony and beauty in order to embrace the source and goal of love, harmony and beauty which has attracted the soul through all planes.

And as the soul has approached nearer, so much closer it has been drawn. It is the unveiling of that radiant garment, which is the body of the soul in the angelic heaven, that brings it to its real destination, the goal which it has continually sought either consciously or unconsciously. Verily, "From God every soul comes, and to God is his return."[50]

What will be the mystery hidden behind the accomplishment of all desire in the next world? Will power with optimism. It is the conviction which is called *yakeen* by the Sufis that will be the guiding light which will illuminate the path of the soul in the spiritual world. What will hinder the progress of the spirits is the lack of the same; though it is not necessary that the soul who has been pessimistic here must remain pessimistic in the next world. It is possible that its journey onward will bring about a change once the soul becomes acquainted with the mysteries of hopefulness.

In what way will the spirits communicate with one another? It is not that all spirits will necessarily communicate; only those spirits who wish to communicate will do so.

In what language? In their own language. If spirits do not know one another's language in the spirit world, there will not be such a difficulty as on the earth, for there is one common language of that plane, a language of the spirit.

* * *

Question: *Will you explain the sentence: "The soul has sought the goal consciously or unconsciously."*

Answer: As it approaches closer, the more conscious it becomes, because the goal is now within its horizon.

Question: *Is there a relationship between the body of the soul on the different planes? Is a higher body in every sense formed from the body of the lower plane?*

Answer: There is a relationship between bodies of the souls on the different planes, certainly. Because they borrow their clay from that particular clay where they are, and there comes the connection caused by that clay, that matter, which is taken.

Yes, a higher body is formed on the design of that, because it is the continuation. For instance, after coming on the earth the soul continues the same life. There is no definite breaking. Therefore, there is something of the earth which can be taken. All cannot be taken, or the souls would have taken not only their bodies, but their houses also.

We shall know more there than here, because that is the plane where knowledge is possible which is not possible here. Do we not say to our friends here, "I cannot understand you. You are a mystery to me"? Perhaps you have been with him for fifty years. That mystery becomes known, that knot is unraveled, as one goes further. For instance, the language of the spheres of the *jinns* is more indistinct compared with the language of the earth, and yet more expressive. And the language of the sphere of the angels is still less distinct and even more expressive than that of the *jinn*.

It is this mystery which can be found in that miracle of the descending of the Holy Ghost. It is not in the outer sense of the explanation that the apostles knew the language of all the people in the world. They knew the language of the soul, and that language of the soul expresses more than the language of people on the earth.

Question: *What does the story of building the tower of Babel mean?*

Answer: The building of a tower is the collecting of mind. When the mind, which is brought from the world of the *jinn*, is filled with the impressions of names and forms gathered on the earth, then a tower is built. When this tower is built, everyone knows his own language from the country from which he has come.

Question: *What is meant in the Old Testament by the giants who were fighting with the gods?*

Answer: The prophets and seers have come time after time, and the people have battled with them and disputed with them, and brought them to all sorts of grief and difficulties. When there is an angelic quality that a person possesses a little more than his fellow men, then there is always a war raised against him. In every way he is pulled down, either criticized, or cruelly treated; all sorts of ill doings and insults come upon the one who shows perhaps a little more of the angelic qualities than average persons. And giants are born of the angels. All human beings are the same, born of the angels. Every human being has already an angel's soul in him.

Question: *In the account of his mystical journey to the angelic heaven, Dante tells how he enters the sphere of the moon, and he calls it a sphere of solid light. Is that an imagining?*

Answer: No, it is in support of that which has been given this day, that the angels are of luminous body, as solid, as concrete as the light one sees. It is his own vision of this plane. The sphere of the moon is the sphere of harmony, because the moon responds to the sun. It is the respondent attitude of the moon which is harmonious. Therefore, it is the sphere of harmony which is heaven.

THE SOUL'S JOURNEY

Conclusion

Conclusion

W̲HAT IS this journey[51], taken by the soul from the source to the manifestation, and from manifestation again to the same source, which is its goal? Is it a journey or is it not a journey? It is a journey in fact and not a journey in truth. It is the change of experiences which makes it a story, and yet the whole story, produced as a moving picture, is on one film, which does not travel for miles and miles as it is seen on the screen. Is it many who journey, or one? It is many while still in illusion, and it is one when the spirit has disillusioned itself. Who journeys, is it the man or God? Both and yet one—two ends of one line.

What is the nature and character of this manifestation? It is an interesting dream. What is this illusion caused by? By cover upon cover, so the soul is covered by a thousand covers. Do these covers give happiness to the soul? Not happiness, but intoxication. The further the soul is removed from its source, the greater its intoxication. Does this intoxication suffice the purpose of the soul and of its journey? It does in a way, but the purpose of the soul is in its longing. And what is that longing for? Sobriety. And how is that sobriety attained? By throwing away the covers which have covered the soul and have thus divided it from its real source and goal.

What does uncover the soul from these covers of illusion? The change which is called death. Either this change, which we call death, is forced upon one against one's desire, which is the most disagreeable experience; it is like snatching away the bottle of drink from the drunken man, which is for the time often disagreeable to him. Or, the other way is that at

263

Conclusion

will this change is brought about, and the soul throws off
the cover that surrounds it. By that it attains the same experience of sobriety, even if it be a glimpse of it, the same
experience which after millions and millions of years, the
soul, drunken by this illusion, arrives at, and yet not exactly
the same experience. The soul, drawn by the magnetic
power of the Divine Spirit, falls into it with a joy inex-
pressible in words, as a loving heart lays itself down in the
arms of its beloved. The intoxication of this joy is so great
that nothing the soul ever experienced in its life makes it so
unconscious of the self as this joy does. But this
unconsciousness of the self in reality becomes the true self-
consciousness. It is then that the soul fully realizes that "I
exist."

The soul who arrives at this stage of realization of consciousness has a different experience. The difference is of
one person having been pulled back, his back turned to the
source, and another person having journeyed towards the
goal, enjoying at every step each experience that it met with
and rejoicing at every moment of this journey approaching
nearer to the goal. What does this soul, conscious of its
progress towards the goal, realize? It realizes, with every
cover it throws off itself, a better life, a greater power, an
increased inspiration, until it arrives at a stage, after having
passed through the planes of the spirit world, the spheres of
the *jinn,* and the heavens of the angels, where the soul
realizes the error which it had known and yet had not
known fully, that error whereby it had identified itself with
its reflection, with its shadows falling on the different
planes.[52]

Neither on the earth plane was man his own self, nor in
the sphere of *jinns,* nor in the heavens of the angels. He was
only a captive of his own illusion caught in a frame, and yet
he was not inside it. It was only his reflection. But he saw
himself nowhere, so he could only identify himself with his
various reflections until he realizes now that "I was what I
am, and I will be what I was. It was I who was, if there were
any, and it is I who will be, if there will be any; it is I who

am the source, the traveler and the goal of this whole existence."

Verily, truth is all the religion there is, and it is truth which will save.

* * *

Question: *From where does the soul come which appears in the angelic sphere and goes into manifestation; and to where does the returning soul go, after leaving the angel sphere?*

Answer: From the spirit of God it comes, and to the light of God it goes.

Question: *Does the soul travel many times from the angelic spheres to the earth and to the angel spheres, or from God via earth to God? Does the soul never come more than once?*

Answer: When the soul is disillusioned and finds, "It was my reflection and not me."

Question: *Would you please explain a little more how, if God is the goal and final attainment, that the traveler, the source and the goal is the "I," that is, the soul itself?*

Answer: Not only the soul itself, even God himself.

Notes

1. Thirteenth century wandering Sufi whose encounter with Jelaluddin Rumi was transformative in Rumi's life, and prompted his poetic career. In Persian, *Shams* means *sun*.

2. Designates Prophet Muhammad.

3. A poet who wrote in Persian, Jelaluddin Rumi (d.1273) is widely known in the Islamic world and has received increasing attention in the West due to many recent translations and versions of his poetry in English. Rumi's works include the *Divani Shamsi Tabriz* and the *Mathnawi*. He is the founder of a Sufi order called the Mevlevi, popularly known as the Whirling Dervishes.

4. The questioner is referring to a lecture given on July 23, 1923, later classified as *Gatha III number 9—Tasawwuf (Metaphysics)*.

5. These are among the seven grades of initiation recognized by the Sufis of the members of the spiritual hierarchy. For further elaboration, see *The Unity of Religious Ideals*, Sufi Order Publications, New Lebanon NY, 1979 (140–142).

6. The original comment is on page 28. See also the last paragraph in the lecture in chapter 43, on page 210.

7. Genesis 32:24–30

8. The Prophet Muhammad's mission lasted for twenty three years, from 610 to 632; he was sixty-three when he died.

9. Matthew 5:5

10. One of the seven grades of initiates in the spiritual hierarchy, whose will has come close to the divine will. See note 5.

11. According to tradition, whenever anyone climbed the wall of mystery and looked over at the other side, he smiled and jumped over, never to return. Once, when a certain person was climbing the wall, the people tied his feet with seven chains to prevent his jumping over. When he looked over the other side, he smiled, but

when he was hauled down, he had lost his power of speech. Inayat Khan's interpretation of this mystery has a bearing on the conclusion of this book. "The one who has seen the other side of the wall, to him all things that the people attach great importance and value to seem nothing. For that person truth and fact are two things. For everybody else truth and fact are the same. ... The light of truth falling upon the facts makes them disappear." (This lecture, titled *The Word That Was Lost,* was given in December 1922. A highly edited version was published in the series *The Sufi Message of Hazrat Inayat Khan,* Volume II, 1962, 1973.)

12. The seventh–eighth century philosopher Shankaracharya was the celebrated teacher of the Vedanta philosophy of non-duality (*advaita*).

13. Pir-o-Murshid Inayat Khan gave a series of lectures on the personality, originally published as *Character Building and The Art of Personality.* This material has been re-edited and presented as *Creating the Person: A Practical Guide to the Development of Self* (Omega Publications, 1995). These lectures on personality were originally given during the summer of 1923, alternating with the lectures on the soul. We see in this passage the complementarity of the two themes.

14. Actually a *hadith* of the Prophet Muhammad.

15. Herod (the Great) was king of Judea from 40–4 BCE; he was notorious for his massacre of the innocents in Bethlehem.

16. The questioner refers to a lecture given on August 20, 1923, published in *Creating the Person* in the chapter entitled "Complaining and Smiling."

17. In Helen M. Luke's book *Kaleidoscope: The Way of Woman,* published by Parabola Books in 1992, there is a striking similarity in Luke's observation that "One of the basic qualities of the feminine psyche is its capacity for total devotion" (38).

18. "Greek philosophers" may have been said.

19. The following day, during a lecture on the subject of gratefulness, an aspect of the personality, someone asked, "What is the highest perception of freedom?" Inayat Khan answered, "The highest perception of freedom comes when a person has freed himself from the false ego, when he is no longer what he was. All different manner of freedom, for the moment that gives a sensation of freedom. The true freedom is in oneself; when one's soul is free, then there is nothing in this world that binds us. Everywhere one

Notes

will breathe freedom, in the heaven and on earth." See *Creating the Person*, p.53.

20. In fact, this question had been asked a few days earlier by someone in the audience. See the question and answer section of chapter 15 on page 85.

21. Two of the prominent editors of this material have silently changed *malakut* to *jabrut* (*jabarut*) in earlier published editions. But since Inayat Khan is consistent in his use of *malakut* to refer to one's experience of one's own world within, I have left it *malakut* as originally stated.

22. *The Mysticism of Sound* was first published in 1923. It is reprinted in *The Sufi Message of Hazrat Inayat Khan*, Vol. 2 (London: Barrie and Jenkins, 1962; rpt. 1973).

23. Matthew 7:14

24. The play *Una*, produced during the Summer School towards the end of August, was begun by Pir-o-Murshid Inayat Khan in June of 1923 on board the S.S. Olympic. The play's theme is transformation, a Pygmalion story in which a woman artist's statue comes to life. For the text of the play, see *The Sufi Message of Hazrat Inayat Khan*, Vol. 12 (London: Barrie Books, 1960).

25. Mir Mahbub Ali Khan, the Nizam of Hyderabad, at whose court Inayat Khan sang and played the vina as a young man.

26. Perhaps this is a reference to Jelaluddin Rumi's *Mathnawi*, a masterpiece of Persian poetry in rhyming couplets, presenting mystical teaching through stories and anecdotes. See nn.1 and 3.

27. Kabir (1440–1518), Indian poet and mystic who attempted to unite Hindu and Muslim thought; he preached the essential unity of all religions.

28. Inayat Khan calls "the word that was lost" a symbolical phrase, a paradox, to account for something which at first is missing and then appears as the seer progresses. By this phrase is not meant a word which is audible only to the ears; but rather all that is expressed and comes as a revelation. By knowing revelation, one accomplishes the purpose of life, and the word which was lost is found.

29. For more information on alchemy, see Titus Burckhardt's *Alchemy*, (Penguin Books, 1971), originally published in German in 1960.

30. See nn. 11 and 28

Notes

31. Ecclesiastes 1:9

32. Ralph Waldo Emerson (1803–1882), lecturer, poet, and essayist, was a leading exponent of New England Transcendentalism along with Henry David Thoreau and others.

33. Matthew 7:1

34. This lecture was originally intended to be included in the first edition of *The Soul Whence and Whither*. A note in the margin initially classified this lecture as Metaphysics VII. The note was crossed out and this lecture was not put in the first edition, or in any other edition of this material. (This lecture, without the questions and answers, has been published in the *Gatha* series.) Because of the relevance of the topic, it has been included in this edition.

35. A few days later, Inayat Khan gave a full lecture on the subject of the will, titled "*Qaza* and *Qadr*: the will, human and divine." This lecture was published in the book *The Unity of Religious Ideals*.

36. See nn. 1 and 3.

37. *The Phenomenon of the Soul* was written by Sherifa Lucy Goodenough, and published in 1919.

38. Chapters 25 through 35 are those ten lectures on Metaphysics plus an additional lecture, originally intended to be part of this grouping, included here as chapter 33, making the total eleven. See n. 34.

39. An earlier edition of this material inserts this sentence into the text at this point: The Sufi poets have pictured these three in their verse as *bagh, bahar* and *bulbul*—the garden, the spring and the nightingale.

40. Qur'an 96:8

41. This question concerning the different kinds of space, as well as the next question, using the phrase "a rapid run," refer to themes raised in Chapter 24 (both in the lecture and the questions and answers). Chronologically, that earlier chapter immediately precedes this chapter. But, following the practice of the editor of the first edition, I have included the additional lectures on the subject of manifestation given earlier that summer in Part II. See note 38.

42. See note 22.

43. In the Persian story of Hatim, a princess made the condition

that she would marry only the one who could bring her a desired pearl that she longed to have. Hatim, whose work it was to roam the countryside and help those in need, found a lover of the princess most unhappy because he could not find that pearl. After great difficulty, Hatim brought the pearl to the princess, and she consented to accept Hatim as her lover. Hatim said that this promise must be granted to his friend, who was really her lover, and that Hatim was the lover of those who were in need.

44. One of the members of the audience, who also took down the lectures and the questions and answers, Sirdar van Tuyll, made note at this point, "Love of territory has caused many deaths and what you love you must get."

45. John 11

46. Genesis 22

47. Milkmaids who lived in the wood Vandravana (Brindavan) on the left bank of the Jumna in India, where Krishna in the character of gopala, or cowherd, spent his youth.

48. A version of this story is also presented in chapter 31, on page 157.

49. Acts 17:28

50. Qur'an 96:8

51. Both this last lecture—the conclusion—and the first lecture—the introduction—were actually given on the same day, at the end of this series. The reader might find it interesting to look again, at this point, at the introduction, a lecture which immediately preceded the conclusion when given on 19 September 1923. The introduction, and the questions and answers which follow it, also have a certain resonance in this position in the series of lectures.

52. At this point, Sophia Saintsbury Green noted down on one of the manuscripts, "As the sun had thought by looking at the sunflower 'I am the sunflower,' forgetting at that moment that the sunflower was only its footprint."

INDEX

273

Index

inharmony
  and illness, 173
  between mind and body, 171
  see also harmony
inheritance, 113
initiation, 25–27
innocence, 23, 65, 126
  of childhood lost, 94
inspiration, 5, 29, 35f., 41, 116, 264
intelligence, 159, 186
  and knowledge, 185
intention, 165
interest, 69, 191
intoxication, 252
  and happiness, 263
intuition, 36, 74, 83, 179
Iris, 139, 141
jabrut, 118, 241
Jacob, 40
jazz, 236
jelal, 40
jemal, 40
Jesus Christ, *see* Christ
jinn, 57, 63
  communication with, 78
jinn plane, 101
  exchange of qualities on, 233
jinn sphere, 211
jinn world, 63, 200
jnanan, 58
journey
  of the soul, 263
  speed of, 195
  joy in, 214
  map of, 72
Judgement Day, 206
justice, 99, 168, 206, 224, 227, 234
  God's, 200–203
Kabir, 144
karma, 43, 99, 102, 164, 202, 234

Index

Note on Glossary

The foreign words used in the text are generally explained at the time they are introduced. Readers who desire more technical definitions of these words will be able to find them in the glossary included in the volume *Complete Works of Pir-o-Murshid Hazrat Inayat Khan, Lectures 1923 II*. All of the material in the present volume has been edited based upon the text of this volume in the *Complete Works* series. The volumes of that series are available from Omega Publications, and interested readers are encouraged to contact the publisher.

INAYAT KHAN: BIOGRAPHICAL NOTE

Pir-o-Murshid Inayat Khan (1882–1927), founder of the Sufi Order International, came to the West as a representative of the highest musical traditions of his native India. He brought with him a message of love, harmony, and beauty that was both the quintessence of Sufi teaching and a revolutionary approach to the harmonizing of Western and Eastern spirituality.

Inayat Khan dedicated his early life to the mastery of the subtle intricacies of classical Indian music, winning the high title of Tansen from the Nizam of Hyderabad, a powerful ruler and renowned patron of the musical arts.

In the fulfillment of his quest for a spiritual teacher, Inayat Khan took initiation from Shaykh al-Mashaykh Sayed Muhammed Abu Hashim Madani. While Madani was an initiator of the four main Sufi lineages in India, his primary connection was with the Chishti Order. At the end of Inayat Khan's apprenticeship, his teacher enjoined him to travel to the West and harmonize the spiritualities of East and West.

On September 13 of 1910 Inayat Khan began an odyssey that would encompass three continents and transform the lives of thousands. He eventually settled in in Suresnes, a suburb of Paris. During his sixteen years in the West, he created a school of spiritual training based upon the traditional teachings of the Chishti Sufis and infused with a revolutionary vision—a vision of the unity of religious ideals and the awakening of humanity to the divinity within.